"Everything begins and ends with respect."
Samurai Code

Andrew Matthews has been writing for fun since he was seven, but was a teacher for twenty-three years before becoming a full-time author. He has written over sixty books for children and teenagers, including *Cat Song*, which was nominated for the Smarties Book Prize in 1994, and the critically acclaimed *Love Street*. He is a hugely versatile writer, and has retold many myths, legends and classic stories, as well as creating his own original picture books and novels.

Andrew lives in Reading with his wife and their cat.

THE
WAY
OF THE
WARRIOR

Andrew Matthews

USBORNE

For Spooky
with love and thanks for the time we shared

Editorial consultant: Tony Bradman

First published in the UK in 2007 by Usborne Publishing Ltd., Usborne House, 83-85 Saffron Hill, London EC1N 8RT, England. www.usborne.com
Copyright © Andrew Matthews, 2007

Cover illustration by Yuko.

A CIP catalogue record for this book is available from the British Library.

JFMAMJ ASOND/07 ISBN 9780746076354 Printed in Great Britain.

Author's Note

In sixteenth century Japan, a "family" was roughly equivalent to a modern Scottish clan, and people customarily stated their family name before their given name.

Some of the incidents in this story are based upon the battle of Mikata ga Hara, which took place in 1572. I have also "borrowed" some characters from history, such as Tokugawa Ieyasu, who went on to become supreme ruler of Japan in 1600, and founded a dynasty that lasted more than two hundred years.

Characters

SHIMOMURA FAMILY
Lord Kensu
Lady Izanami
Jimmu

Lord Kensu's samurai bodyguard
Araki Nichiren

CHOJU FAMILY
Lord Ankan
Lady Murasaki
Lady Takeko

Lord Ankan's guard
Captain Ishida Muraki
Sergeant Hankei (drill instructor)
Guardsman Kambei
Guardsman Kanji
Guardsman Hisashi
Guardsman Sadamichi
Ina Kyo (samurai instructor)

LORD ANKAN'S ALLIES
Lord Tokugawa Ieyasu
Lord Oda Nobunaga
General Ietada
General Tadakatsu
General Kazumasa

THE ENEMY
Lord Takeda Shingen

BANDITS
Toshiro (bandit leader)
Buzen
Kichi

Prologue

Shimomura family home

SURUGU PROVINCE, SPRING 1565

Jimmu was dreaming. In the dream, a white cloud in the sky was calling him by name. Then the cloud vanished as he woke up. It was late at night. One of the screen doors in his room had been left open, and an oblong of moonlight lay across the floor. From the garden outside came the sound of water splashing on stones, and the whirr and chirrup of insects.

"Jimmu!" said a voice. "You must get up."

Jimmu turned and saw Nichiren standing over him. Araki Nichiren was his father's most trusted samurai bodyguard, but Jimmu did not like him. Nichiren was short and stocky. His head was shaved down to white stubble, except for a tightly tied pigtail. He always spoke gruffly and never seemed to be in a good mood.

Jimmu yawned and pulled a face.

"I was dreaming," he said. "I dreamed that—"

"This is no time for nonsense," said Nichiren. "On your feet, and hurry! Lord Kensu has asked for you."

The mention of his father's name brought Jimmu fully awake. Lord Kensu was not a man it paid to keep waiting.

Jimmu followed Nichiren through the house, to the main room of his father's apartment. All the lanterns had been lit and moths were circling them. Lord Kensu was seated on a raised platform at the far end of the room. His suit of armour rested on a stand beside him. The helmet was topped by a strip of metal, shaped like a crescent moon. On the wall beside Lord Kensu hung the banner of the Shimomura family, showing a golden crab with raised claws. The same design was embroidered on the lapels of Lord Kensu's black silk kimono. On the floor, directly in front of him, was a dagger in a red scabbard.

Jimmu bowed to his father.

"Sit close to me, Jimmu," said Lord Kensu. "I want to see your face."

Jimmu crossed the room and sat two arms' lengths from his father.

Lord Kensu looked at his son for longer than he had

ever looked at him before. Jimmu looked back, and saw sorrow in his father's eyes.

At last, Lord Kensu said, "How old are you, Jimmu?"

"Ten," said Jimmu.

Lord Kensu sighed.

"You are too young to understand, but listen to me carefully and do as I tell you," he said. "You will leave this house tonight, and you will never return. You will not see me or your mother again in this life."

Jimmu could not take in his father's words. How could Jimmu possibly leave and never see his parents again? The house was where they all lived.

Lord Kensu looked down at the dagger, and when he spoke again his voice was thick with shame.

"I have brought disgrace on our family," he said. "So much disgrace that the Emperor has decreed that the name Shimomura no longer exists, and all my property must be forfeited. I cannot bear such humiliation, and I have no choice but to commit seppuku."

An expression of pride crossed Lord Kensu's face.

"My wife, your mother, Lady Izanami has gone

on before me to prepare my place," he said. "I am looking forward to joining her."

Jimmu frowned.

"Where will you join her, Father, and what is seppuku?" he asked.

Lord Kensu loosened the belt of his kimono, opened the robe and pressed his hand against his stomach.

"This is the centre of my body, where my spirit lives," he said. "Only by cutting myself open can I show others that my spirit remains courageous and pure in the face of dishonour. When Nichiren judges that my agony is too great for me to stand, he will put an end to my suffering."

Jimmu's head whirled. What was his father saying? How could he talk so calmly about agony?

"When it is over, you must go with Nichiren," Lord Kensu said. "He will take care of you."

"Caring for your son will be a privilege, My Lord," said Nichiren.

"What will you tell him about me, Nichiren?" Lord Kensu enquired softly.

Jimmu noticed the two men exchange a look that he could not fathom.

"I will tell him as much as he needs to know, My Lord," said Nichiren.

Lord Kensu nodded, then picked up the dagger and unsheathed it.

This can't be real! Jimmu told himself. This is another dream.

He saw the dagger flash, saw dark blood spurt in the lantern light. He heard the hoarse, strangled noise of his father holding back a scream.

Nichiren stepped forwards, drew his sword with both hands and swept the blade up towards Lord Kensu's neck.

Jimmu shut his eyes.

Something thudded onto the floorboards.

Jimmu tried to believe that, if he kept his eyes closed for long enough, he could unmake what had happened, but it was too true to be unmade.

Nichiren led Jimmu into the garden. Jimmu no longer recognized his surroundings or himself. Something inside him had frozen. He was not even aware that he was crying, until Nichiren barked, "Stop snivelling!"

The harshness of his tone made Jimmu start; a sob turned to a hiccup.

"Listen to me, boy!" Nichiren growled. "Your father has committed seppuku. Your mother drank poison and died an hour ago. You have no parents and no home. All you have is me. I'm your father now."

"Yes, Nichiren," said Jimmu.

Nichiren glowered. "What was that?"

"Yes...Father."

"That's better," said Nichiren. "Always call me Father from now on, and never tell anyone your family name. The soft life is over for you, boy. We're going to pick out two horses from the stables, and then we'll ride away from here."

Jimmu was struggling to grasp what it was that had caused his world to change so completely, but when he tried to put together the words to ask Nichiren, all he could manage was, "Why?"

"Lord Choju Ankan is why, boy," Nichiren told him. "He is a greedy, cruel demon of a man, who cares for nobody but himself. Your father offended him a long time ago, and Lord Ankan never forgot. He accused your father of plotting to murder the

Emperor, and produced false papers to prove it. The Emperor has proclaimed your father a traitor."

Nichiren trembled with rage. Flecks of foam formed in the corners of his mouth.

"Lord Ankan caused the death of your parents, and took away your home," he continued. "Whenever you're cold, or tired, or hungry, remember that it's Lord Ankan's fault. You must learn to hate him. One day you will avenge your father by killing Lord Ankan. I will teach you how. Until then, your father's unquiet spirit will be forced to wander the earth. Only you can bring him rest. You understand?"

Jimmu's head was whirling. "No," he said. "I don't understand."

Nichiren grunted.

"Your understanding isn't necessary," he said. "For the moment, all you have to do is obey."

Nichiren turned, and marched into the night.

Jimmu stumbled after him.

Chapter 1

OWARI PROVINCE, SUMMER 1572

For the past six weeks, the bandits had done well for themselves. There were ten of them, not much of a gang compared to some, but their leader, Toshiro, was as sly as a monkey. Like most of his men, Toshiro had been a foot soldier, until he fought on the losing side in a battle. The defeat took away his living quarters and his livelihood. Battles still went on, but Toshiro and the others took no part in them. With the Emperor virtually powerless, Japan was in the hands of the great warlords, and they were locked in a deadly struggle for supremacy.

Toshiro had picked the gang's latest hideout in a forest that lay close to a main road. Kyoto, the city where the Emperor lived, was only two days' journey to the west, and the road was busy. The forest provided plenty of cover for the bandits. They could charge out from, and melt back into the trees.

Toshiro had been cautious, not stealing too much, not killing too many, but he knew that the gang would soon have to move on. They had become a nuisance, and their reputation might have spread as far as Kyoto. Though the Emperor was weak, his Imperial Guard remained formidable, and for days Toshiro had been anticipating an unwelcome visit from them. He had held on in the hope of a prize rich enough to see the gang through the winter.

That morning, just before sunrise, the prize turned up in the form of an ox cart loaded with casks of rice wine. The driver was in a hurry, and risked an early start on his own instead of travelling in convoy with other merchants. As his luck ran out, the gang's luck was in. They ambushed the driver, trussed him up, and drove him and his cart to a clearing a little way into the forest, to wait for nightfall. It would be safer to take the cart to their camp under cover of darkness. They had not yet decided what to do with the driver, whether to hold him for ransom or slit his throat.

Summer was almost over, but nevertheless, by midday the forest was sweltering. Buzen, a bandit with a bad squint, kept watch, while the others lazed about, chatting or dozing. A few would have loved to crack open a cask and celebrate, but Toshiro had forbidden it and no one dared to disobey.

The driver was seated with his back against one of the cartwheels. He was a skinny man, with a straggly black beard and bulging eyes. The corners of his mouth were pulled down, giving him an expression of pure misery. A rope had been wound around his chest to bind his arms tightly against his sides. Every now and then he rocked forward and back, as if he were trying to comfort himself.

"You won't kill me, will you?" he grizzled, to no one in particular. "I don't deserve to die! Just let me go. I swear I won't tell a soul."

Kichi, a stubble-faced thug who was lying near the cart, aimed a kick at the driver.

"Be quiet!" said Kichi. "I'm trying to sleep."

"Sorry, sir!" the driver squeaked. "I won't speak again. I'll be so quiet that you'll forget I'm here, so quiet that—"

He broke off when he saw Kichi point to the dagger at his waist.

Toshiro sat slightly apart from the others. He was pleased, and his smile resembled the smile on a statue of Lord Buddha. His mind was busy with magic, transforming wine into rice, salt, warm clothing and blankets. He would have liked to buy horses so that the gang could range more freely, but horses were too expensive. Perhaps the gang would be able to steal some mounts on their journey north to their winter hideout in the mountains.

"Someone's coming!" Buzen hissed urgently.

Several of the gang sat upright.

Toshiro's hand clutched the hilt of his sword.

"How many?" he asked.

"One man on foot, alone."

Toshiro relaxed.

"One man?" he said. "He'll probably run like a hare as soon as he sees our ugly mugs, eh, lads?"

A few chuckles greeted his words.

Toshiro relaxed even more when the solitary stranger appeared at the edge of the clearing, because he was a boy of sixteen or seventeen. When he caught sight of the gang, the boy stopped dead in his tracks.

Toshiro slowly stood up and took a good look at the intruder.

The boy was tall and slender. He wore a brown cotton kimono that was faded and travel-worn, and carried a sword in the sash around his waist. The sword had a red lacquer scabbard. The boy's hair had been tied back, revealing a face that was striking rather than handsome. His dark, watchful eyes glanced around the clearing, taking in the bandits, the cart, the captive driver.

Since Toshiro had time on his hands, he decided to have a bit of fun with the lad, who did not seem to pose any threat.

"Lost your way?" Toshiro said.

"No," said the boy. "I'm going to Mitsukage Castle. I was told that I could take a short cut through this forest."

"You were told wrong," Toshiro said. "You'd better go back to the road and ask again."

The boy did not move.

Toshiro frowned, raised his arm and pointed.

"The road is that way," he said.

The boy stayed put.

Stubborn, stupid – or both? wondered Toshiro. He nodded to Kichi, who stood up and brushed dust from his clothes, before ambling over to the intruder.

Kichi looked the boy up and down, and sniggered.

"Does your father really let you play with that big sharp sword?" he said. "He must be as big a fool as you look."

The boy stiffened slightly, but his voice was calm as he said, "I'm not looking for any trouble."

"No?" jeered Kichi. "But what if trouble is looking for you? Think you know how to handle yourself, do you?"

"I don't want to fight you," the boy replied.

Kichi sighed.

"That's a real shame!" he said. "Because me and my friends reckon you've seen a bit too much, so now I'm going to have to kill you."

Kichi's fingers closed around the hilt of his sword, but before the blade had cleared its sheath, the boy drew his own sword and lopped off the bandit's head with a single, graceful stroke.

Uproar broke out in the clearing. Men struggled to their feet and fumbled for weapons.

"Don't let him escape!" yelled Toshiro.

But the boy, it seemed, had no intention of escaping, for instead of fleeing from the bandits, he attacked them. He was everywhere, running, leaping and twirling like a dancer. The blade of his sword glinted in the dappled sunlight.

One bandit died from a blow that almost chopped him in two at the waist; another died before he could notch an arrow onto the string of his bow. A third received a wound in the neck that severed an artery.

Swinging his sword and bellowing like a bull calf, Toshiro bore down on the boy. The boy waited calmly and then, with perfect timing, drove the point of his sword up under Toshiro's ribcage and penetrated his heart.

When the surviving members of the gang saw that their leader was dead, they turned and ran.

"A demon!" one of them shouted. "We were attacked by a demon!"

The boy cleaned his sword on the sleeve of Toshiro's kimono, and approached the driver of the ox cart.

The driver trembled.

"Don't kill me, sir!" he gibbered. "I'm just a poor

tradesman who never hurt anyone!"

"I'm not going to kill you," said the boy. "Lean forwards."

He cut the ropes and freed the driver, who crouched on all fours at his feet.

"Bless you, sir!" the driver sobbed. "May the ancestors shower a thousand—"

"Do you know the way to Mitsukage Castle?" interrupted the boy.

The driver dared to raise his head and peep at his rescuer.

"Keep walking north-east and you'll pick up a drovers' road. Follow it for three days and you'll find Mitsukage Castle. The lord of the castle is—"

"I know who is lord there," said the boy.

The driver kneeled up.

"But first, come with me to Kyoto!" he insisted. "My wine will fetch a good price, and I can reward you for saving my life."

"I don't want money," said the boy, and strode off.

The driver watched until the boy had almost reached the far end of the clearing, then he called out, "Sir! What's your name?"

"Jimmu," said the boy, without looking back. "My name is Jimmu."

As Jimmu walked in the shade of the trees, he thought of Nichiren. Although he had been dead for months, Nichiren was still very much alive in Jimmu's memory. Jimmu had spent seven years being trained by Nichiren, and he knew exactly the kind of comments the old samurai would have made about his actions. If he half closed his eyes, Jimmu could almost see Nichiren marching along beside him – not withered by the wasting illness that had finally killed him, but strong and healthy: the warrior of Jimmu's childhood.

"You lost your temper and behaved rashly!" Nichiren scolded. "It was only necessary for you to kill the bandit leader. The others were a waste of time and effort."

"One of them insulted my father!" protested Jimmu, talking to Nichiren in his head.

"*You* insult your father with your impatience," Nichiren countered. "You have drawn needless attention to yourself. Stick to our plan. No one must know who or what you are. When you arrive at Mitsukage Castle, be humble and polite. Conceal your skill until an opportunity arises, then strike! But be sure that the time is right. Lord Ankan's blood will wash away your father's shame, and you will prove worthy of being called Lord Kensu's son. Your death will be glorious."

"Yes, Nichiren."

"You're talking to yourself!" snapped Nichiren. "Keep your mouth shut and your mind clear, and perhaps you won't die like me, gasping out your last breath on a sickbed. Is that the kind of end you want, boy?"

Jimmu shook his head.

Four days later, at sunset, Jimmu caught his first sight of Mitsukage Castle, though Nichiren had described it so often, it seemed to Jimmu as if he had been there before. The castle was built of wood that had weathered to a silvery grey. Its main tower had two tiers, with roofs that curled up at the edges, so that they resembled the wings of a heron in flight.

Nichiren's voice echoed through Jimmu's mind.

"Mitsukage Castle is a lair, and Lord Choju Ankan is the dragon who lurks inside it. His face is as loathsome as a toad's. His eyes burn with lust for riches and power, and he will stop at nothing to win them. Your father was the best of lords, noble, honourable, fierce in battle and merciful in victory. Ankan is a scheming coward who hides behind the courage of others, waiting for the chance to betray them. Never underestimate his slyness. Believe none of his honeyed words, there's poison in their sweetness. Use the glow of your hatred to see him for what he is. Strike him down for your father's sake, and let your heart be filled with joy."

"I will!" whispered Jimmu.

To reach the main gate of the castle, Jimmu had to cross a bridge over a moat whose waters shone blood-red with light reflected from the sunset sky.

Jimmu beat his fist against the gate.

Almost at once, a spyhole opened, and was filled with the face of the gatekeeper. His expression was unfriendly.

"What d'you want?" he rasped.

Jimmu had practised his answer over and over again.

"I want to serve Lord Choju Ankan," he said. "I want to be a guard here at Mitsukage Castle."

The gatekeeper's laugh wheezed like a pair of bellows.

"A guard?" he said. "Better run along and come back when you're fully grown."

"I want to serve Lord Ankan!" insisted Jimmu.

Another voice said, "What's going on, gatekeeper?"

The gatekeeper's face turned from the spyhole. "Youngster outside reckons he wants to be a guard, sir. He's only a bit of a kid. Shall I see him off, sir?"

There was a moment's pause, then the other voice said, "No. Open up and let me question him."

Bolts thumped and scraped; hinges squealed. The gate opened wide enough for Jimmu to slip through into a courtyard. Directly in front of him stood a short, broad-shouldered man dressed in black armour that shone like a beetle's back. He looked middle aged. He had a broad face and his head was shaven, except for a black pigtail that was streaked with white. At his waist, the man wore the long and short swords of a fully fledged samurai. His air and stance told Jimmu that he was accustomed to being obeyed, and Jimmu bore this in mind throughout all that followed.

"I am Ishida Muraki, captain of Lord Ankan's guards," the man announced. "Who are you?"

"Jimmu, sir."

"What is your family name?"

"I have no family, sir," said Jimmu.

The captain looked Jimmu over, and hobbled slowly round him, limping on his left leg.

"Where have you come from?" he demanded.

"Nagoya," Jimmu replied.

The captain did not need to ask how Jimmu had made the journey. From the state of the boy's feet, he had obviously walked.

"When was your last meal?" asked Captain Muraki.

"Two days ago."

"You must be hungry."

Jimmu held himself proudly.

"I'm no beggar, sir," he said.

The captain grunted approvingly.

"Gatekeeper, take Jimmu to the cookhouse and scrounge what you can for him. Bring him to my quarters when he's finished."

The gatekeeper bowed.

"Am I a guard now, sir?" Jimmu asked the captain.

Captain Muraki smiled at the boy's determination.

"Eat first, then we'll talk and I'll decide," he said.

"Thank you, Captain Muraki," said Jimmu, bowing politely.

Jimmu's interview took place in a long, bare room. It was dusk; the shutters had been lowered and oil lamps lit. The only decorative object in the room was a tall blue vase that stood on a low table set against the wall. The floorboards were so clean and well polished that Jimmu was momentarily aware of how badly he needed a bath, and a change of clothes.

Captain Muraki was seated on a dais. He had replaced his armour with a dark grey silk kimono. Apparently engrossed in reading a scroll, the captain did not react when Jimmu entered, other than to murmur, "Sit down."

Jimmu sat.

The captain continued to read.

"Why do you wish to serve Lord Ankan?" he asked abruptly.

Jimmu understood that Captain Muraki's brisk manner was supposed to catch him unawares, and pretended to be startled.

"Because he is a great general," he blurted.

"And what use would you be to a great general?"

"I can fight, sir."

"That's nothing!" the captain snorted. "Any fool can fight. There are drunken brawls in taverns every day."

"I'm not a fool, sir, and I'm not a drunk," said Jimmu.

Captain Muraki looked up, straight into Jimmu's eyes.

"Lord Ankan has many enemies," he said. "How do I know that you're not spying for one of them?"

Jimmu was prepared for this question, and replied calmly, "If you believed that I was a spy, I would already be under arrest, sir."

Captain Muraki raised a hand to his face to conceal a grin.

"What happened to your family?" he said.

For the first time, Jimmu seemed to behave like an awkward teenager, wriggling and blushing.

"I don't like talking about myself," he mumbled.

"Then learn to like it!" the captain said, and went back to reading the scroll.

Nichiren had made Jimmu rehearse his story until it sounded like the truth, until Jimmu almost believed it himself.

"When I was a baby, I was found abandoned outside the Buddhist monastery at Sengen, between the cities of Nara and Nagoya," he said. "I never knew who my parents were. The monks took me in, and found a wet nurse to care for me. When I was old enough, I learned how to pray and how to meditate. When I was seven or eight, one of the monks, a retired samurai called Soun, took an interest in me. He taught me unarmed combat, and how to use the spear, bow and sword. I'm best with the sword. Soun said I was the most skilled swordsman of my age that he had ever seen. He told me that I have the makings of a samurai."

Captain Muraki was no longer pretending to read; Jimmu had completely captured his attention.

"Soun grew old," Jimmu continued. "In spring, he fell sick. Before he died, he called me to his side and asked me to choose between following the way of Lord Buddha, or the way of the warrior. I chose to be a warrior."

"Why?"

"Because war is everywhere," said Jimmu. "It's the way of the world."

Captain Muraki sighed.

"War has stolen my ability to run," he said. "How much are you prepared to lose, Jimmu?"

"I'm prepared to pay any price," said Jimmu. "After Soun died, I left the monastery, wandered the country and talked to people. That's how I learned about Lord Ankan, and here I am."

Captain Muraki could not be certain how much of Jimmu's story was genuine, but he was impressed with the way the boy had told it.

"Have you killed a man, Jimmu?"

"Yes."

"How did you feel afterwards?"

"Grateful that he didn't kill me," said Jimmu.

The captain gave a satisfied nod.

"I'm giving you the benefit of the doubt, Jimmu," he said. "Tomorrow you will start your training. I'll be watching you closely. Don't let me down."

"I won't, sir."

"You may go now, Jimmu. Ask one of the men outside to tell you where the bunkhouse is."

Jimmu carefully arranged his face into his most winning smile.

"Thank you, Captain Muraki," he said.

ISE PROVINCE, SUMMER 1572

The following morning, after washing and eating, Jimmu visited the quartermaster and was issued with a uniform. He dressed in blue cotton breeches, which tucked into gaiters, a short wrap-over green cotton shirt, and straw sandals. Then he buckled on an armoured breastplate that was decorated with the emblem of the Choju family, a white diamond within a black diamond. Lastly, he put on a pair of armoured gloves, and an iron helmet.

Jimmu had never worn armour before, and felt constrained by it. The straps of the breastplate chafed; the weight of the helmet was like a headache.

These things must be endured, he thought, and he half smiled, because the words were so familiar. He remembered marching at night through summer heat, through rain and snow; going without food for days on end; Nichiren's hard, clipped voice saying, "These things must be endured."

Jimmu found his way to the exercise yard and joined a group of guards who were drilling with spears. The drill instructor, Sergeant Hankei, issued orders in the manner of a dog barking at an intruder.

"Shoulder arms! Present arms! Form ranks!"

Though the drill was tedious, Jimmu was not bored. He withdrew to the quiet place in his mind where nobody could follow. When he was there, his body no longer seemed of any importance, and he did not care how often it had to repeat the same action.

"Shoulder arms! Right turn!"

"Obey orders without question," Nichiren had told him. "Be reliable and conscientious, and in time you'll be taken for granted. No one will take any more notice of you than if you were a floor mat. When you've achieved that, you'll be ready to strike. Be swift, certain, and give no quarter. Choju Ankan's wife is dead and he has not remarried. His mother, Lady Murasaki, lives with him. He has a daughter, Lady Takeko, who is about the same age as you. If you must kill them in order to reach him, so be it. It would be sweet to tell Lord Ankan whose son you are, and listen to him beg for his life. But take no chances. Above all else, be patient!"

The first part of Nichiren's plan had been carried out successfully. Jimmu had joined the guards in Mitsukage Castle. Now he had to fit in.

"Left wheel! Shoulder arms!" shouted Sergeant Hankei.

Jimmu knew that he could stand the drilling, but being patient was going to be difficult. Nichiren had honed him like a weapon, and he was eager to rid the world of Lord Ankan's evil influence.

One of the skills that Jimmu had acquired was the ability to sleep for precisely as long as he chose, and now he woke himself in the middle of the night. While his eyes slowly accustomed themselves to the gloom, his ears sifted the air. He heard the breathing and snoring of the other men around him, a rush of wind beneath the eaves, the eerie call of a night bird.

Jimmu had willed himself to wake because he wished to explore Mitsukage Castle in secret. Nichiren had drummed the castle's layout into him so thoroughly that Jimmu could sketch it from memory, but he was keen to see the reality for himself, and discover what changes might have been made over the past seven years. In particular, he wanted to familiarize himself with the route to Lord Ankan's apartments.

"The cost of perfection is constant practice," Nichiren had told him on countless occasions. "Practise until you no longer have to think about what you're doing. Practise until it becomes as natural as breathing."

Tonight, Jimmu intended to practise the killing of Choju Ankan.

But what if I'm found out? he thought. What if a member of the night watch challenges me?

Excitement and fear caused Jimmu's heart to beat faster.

I am a hunter in the night, he thought. My footstep is silent, my body is invisible.

When he was calm, Jimmu felt for the dagger he had wrapped in a black sash and hidden under his sleeping mat. He got up, and stealthily picked his way between the slumbering guards. Outside in the corridor, he slipped the dagger inside his shirt, and tied the sash around his head, so that only his eyes showed. At the end of the corridor, he mounted a staircase to the upper floor and paused. Somewhere to his left lay the private quarters of the Choju family. In his imagination, Jimmu pictured himself hurrying in the opposite direction, his hands still wet with Lord Ankan's blood, uncoiling a length of rope from around his waist. One end of the rope was attached to a grappling hook, which he secured to the base of a shutter frame. Then he lowered himself down the outer wall of the castle, plunged into the moat, swam across and...

The vision faded away. It was nothing more than a sour joke. There was no escape from Mitsukage Castle, and Jimmu did not expect to leave the place alive.

The sound of approaching footsteps made Jimmu spring across the corridor. He pressed himself tightly against a wooden pillar, and kept as still as possible. The footsteps drew closer; Jimmu held his breath.

A guard passed by, muttering to himself.

"Night duty!" he grumbled. "I ought to be taking it easy at my age."

It would have been easy for Jimmu to leap on the man and slide the edge of the dagger across his throat, but a dead guard was bound to provoke a fuss, and an investigation. Besides, Jimmu baulked at the idea of killing in cold blood for no reason.

He waited beside the pillar until he was sure that the guard was safely out of sight, then continued his reconnaissance.

A few minutes later, Jimmu came in sight of Lord Ankan's sleeping chamber, and he advanced cautiously, in case a creaking floorboard betrayed him. When Lord Ankan was in residence, a detail of his personal bodyguard would be on duty at night. Jimmu wondered how many, and where they would position themselves, and—

"Who are you?"

A burst of shock twisted Jimmu around. His hand flew inside his shirt, and his fingers gripped the hilt of his dagger. Then he faltered. He could hardly believe what he saw.

A girl was seated on a window ledge, in a shaft of moonlight that shone through a partly opened shutter. Her eyes looked black, her face, with its delicate nose and mouth, was as pale as paper. She wore a white robe that was luminous in the moonlight. Her hair was straight and glossily dark.

"Are you a ghost?" Jimmu gasped.

The girl sniggered, and tossed her head. Her hair whispered against her shoulders.

"Answer my question first!" she said haughtily. "Who are you?"

"Guardsman Jimmu."

"What are you doing in the private quarters?"

"Er, training!" blurted Jimmu. "A good guard must be alert at all times, and I was testing how alert I am at night."

"Why is that sash wrapped around your face?"

Panic made Jimmu's mind nimble.

"I have a sore throat," he said, pretending to be hoarse. "I was protecting it from the cool night air."

"Take it off!" the girl commanded. "I can hardly make out a word you say."

Jimmu obeyed without question. The girl had a kind of natural authority that was difficult to resist.

When the scarf was undone, the girl peered critically at Jimmu.

"I haven't seen you before," she remarked.

"I'm a new recruit," said Jimmu, "but I'm keen for promotion. That's why I'm training so late."

"Am I pretty?" the girl enquired.

Jimmu was bewildered by the sudden change of subject.

"Pretty?" he said. "I don't know anything about things like that."

The girl heaved a petulant sigh.

"Obviously not!" she said. "In a story, a suitor would tell me that my skin is as smooth as a peach, and my eyes are as beautiful as poems. Guess who I am."

"Why?"

"Because I told you to!" snapped the girl. "And hurry up, before I get bored and shout for the guards. If I tell them that you touched me, they'll take you away and torture you."

"Why would I touch you?" Jimmu said with a frown.

The girl rolled her eyes. "Oh, never mind! Go on, guess who I am."

"A maidservant?" Jimmu ventured.

Annoyance flashed in the girl's eyes, and then her expression turned wistful. "A maidservant," she repeated. "You know, there are times when..." She hesitated, her lips twitched and the annoyance came back into her eyes. "Leave at once!" she commanded. "Commoners are forbidden to enter the private quarters, unless they have been directly summoned. If I find you sneaking around here again, I'll inform my father."

"Your father?" said Jimmu.

The girl straightened her shoulders, and raised her chin.

"My father is Lord Ankan," she announced. "I am Lady Takeko."

"Forgive me, My Lady!" begged Jimmu. "I didn't know. I—"

Lady Takeko waved him away.

Jimmu backed his way along the corridor, bowing continuously. He turned a corner, straightened up and blew out a long breath.

That was a lucky escape! he thought. You were so clumsy and careless, you let a girl catch you out. You'll have to do a lot better than that.

His emotions were tangled. He felt angry at himself, relieved that Lady Takeko had seemed to believe him, insulted by her arrogance, and another feeling, one that he could not identify.

Forget her! he thought. Don't think about her again. Remember, you may have to kill her one day.

Six days after Jimmu's encounter with Lady Takeko, Lord Ankan rode in through the outer gates of Mitsukage Castle, accompanied by his personal bodyguard of four samurai, each with a stern expression and watchful eyes.

Jimmu was among the guards lining the bridge across the moat. They stood to attention with shouldered spears, right hands held across their chests in a welcoming salute.

This is the man who robbed you of your parents and your home, Jimmu thought. This is the man who took away the life you might have had, without a care. This is the greedy demon who ate your childhood. He struggled to control the anger and loathing that surged inside him.

Lord Ankan was encased in black armour. His iron breastplate had been engraved with the Choju emblem. His helmet was topped by a piece of white metal shaped into a pair of horns. Except for his eyes, his face was concealed behind a black-lacquered mask, its features twisted into a warlike grimace. He resembled an insect with a metal carapace. He was a man forged from iron, with a hard, unfeeling heart.

You're going to kill him, Jimmu thought. Your face is the last thing he'll see before he dies. The last thing he'll hear will be your voice, whispering your father's name.

He held himself erect as Lord Ankan's horse trotted by.

Chapter 4
Mitsukage Castle
ISE PROVINCE, SUMMER 1572

Though he had resolved to do otherwise, Jimmu often found his thoughts turning to Lady Takeko in the days that followed. The memory of her face returned to haunt him at unexpected moments. She was, he came to realize, more than pretty, and this was a puzzle to him. How could an evil monster of a man like Choju Ankan father such a beautiful daughter? True, she was spoiled and arrogant, but could there be darker sides to her nature? Was a malevolent being concealed behind her lovely face?

Jimmu had little experience of females. When the other guards discussed women, Jimmu felt embarrassed and ignorant. He did not understand the jokes they made about the maidservants in the castle, and the peasant women in the outlying farms.

"Keep all your dealings with the opposite sex as

brief as possible," was the only advice on the subject that Nichiren had ever offered. "Too much female company turns a man soft."

Jimmu did not stop to reflect why he asked himself so many questions about Takeko, or why he had recurring dreams about her. He was not yet aware of how far their encounter had disturbed him. Lady Takeko – or Jimmu's idea of Lady Takeko – began to fascinate him.

Jimmu settled into his new life. He kept himself to himself, only spoke when he was spoken to, and got to know his fellow guards by watching and listening.

Jimmu was the newcomer, and so became the butt of practical jokes. He was expecting this, since Nichiren had told him what life in a barracks was like. The most important thing was not to overreact: if he lost his temper and made a fuss, it would only encourage the jokers to play more tricks. So he did not complain if he was sent on a false errand. When his sleeping mat was stolen, he rested on the bare floorboards; when cockroaches were sneaked into his mess bowl, he removed them and carried on eating. Before long, the pranks started to tail off. At heart, the guards were a decent enough bunch – with two notable exceptions: Hisashi and Sadamichi.

Hisashi was a musketeer of medium height. His nose veered over towards the right side of his face; his two front teeth were long and yellow, like a rat's. He was a coarse man, who ate noisily, cursed foully and told crude jokes. He thought it was funny to break wind loudly, especially at night.

One evening, Hisashi entered the mess for supper, and sat across the way from Jimmu. Hisashi sniffed at the rice and vegetables in his bowl and grinned.

"This is the life!" he said to Jimmu.

Jimmu did not respond.

Hisashi raised his voice. "This is the life!"

"If you say so," murmured Jimmu.

"I do say so, and I'll tell you why," Hisashi said. "This time last year I was busting my back working on a farm, up to my neck in pig muck, or in a paddy field up to my knees in muddy water. I used to wake before dawn and go to bed at sunset. My life was nothing but grief, see? But it all changed the day I learned how to fire a gun. Now I eat better, sleep better, and earn better money. And it's all thanks to Saya."

"Saya?" Jimmu said uncertainly.

"My gun," explained Hisashi. "I named her after my dead wife. D'you know what the best thing about Saya is?"

"What?" Jimmu said.

"She makes me as good as any fancy samurai!" declared Hisashi. "He can wear expensive armour, and come charging at me on a thoroughbred horse, but I can send him to join his ancestors before he gets anywhere near me."

Hisashi raised his left haunch and broke wind.

"You're right, Hisashi," said a sarcastic voice. "Any samurai who laid eyes on you would instantly recognize you as his equal."

The voice belonged to Sadamichi. Sadamichi was a tall young man with a bony face. His eyes had a slight squint. Sadamichi's vanity showed in his neatly trimmed moustache, which he had grown in imitation of Lord Oda Nobunaga, the famous warlord. He considered himself to be a good deal better than his colleagues, and treated them with contempt.

"That big mouth of yours is going to land you in big trouble one of these days, Sadamichi!" snapped Hisashi.

Sadamichi's smile was thin and mocking.

"Would you care to try shutting it, Hisashi?" he said.

Hisashi scowled. Sadamichi had a reputation as a swordsman, and Hisashi feared him.

"You may be able to shoot a matchlock, Hisashi, but you still stink of the farmyard," jibed Sadamichi. He glanced at Jimmu. "Peasants should be kept in the fields where they belong, don't you agree?"

Jimmu struggled to keep his temper. He detested bullies like Sadamichi.

"I asked you if you agreed with me," said Sadamichi. "Are you stupid, or deaf?"

Jimmu no longer trusted himself. Without a word he stood, and walked out of the mess hall.

"These things must be endured!" he whispered under his breath. "These things must be endured!"

He repeated the sentence over and over, until he felt calm.

Jimmu soon became aware that he had made a serious mistake. By trying to avoid trouble, he had embraced it. The incident in the mess hall had brought him to Sadamichi's attention and, on a whim, Sadamichi singled Jimmu out for special treatment. As far as he was concerned the boy was young, inexperienced and unsure of himself – a perfect victim – and Sadamichi set out to demonstrate his superiority. What he actually demonstrated was his own childishness.

His campaign began with name-calling. When he passed Jimmu deep in the castle's labyrinth of corridors, he whispered, "Farm Boy!" or "Dung Head!" If Jimmu sat anywhere near him in the mess hall, Sadamichi pulled a face, held his nose, and said things like, "I thought Hisashi stank, but the smell of Farm Boy is enough to put you off your food!"

Jimmu knew that Sadamichi was trying to provoke him and did not react, but deep inside his anger glowed like burning charcoal.

The inferno erupted on a day when the air was warm and heavy. The sky was overcast, and all morning distant thunder rumbled in the mountains to the north. It was weather to jangle nerves and set teeth on edge. The castle dogs snapped at anyone who approached them; in the stables, the horses shied, and kicked their stalls.

At noon, Jimmu was relieved of duty and went to the mess hall for his midday meal. About half the guards were present, including Sadamichi.

Sadamichi appeared to be bored. His mess bowl was empty, and he was toying with a chopstick, tossing it up and catching it. When he saw Jimmu, he turned to his neighbour and said loudly, "Lucky I ate before Farm Boy got here!"

Jimmu's anger flared, taking him over so completely that it seemed to be someone else who said, "You talk too much, Sadamichi."

The mess hall fell silent as all conversations ceased.

The thunder sounded louder than before. The storm was on its way.

Sadamichi cocked his head to one side.

"Excuse me, did you say something, Farm Boy?" he asked.

Letting his anger out into the open was so exhilarating that Jimmu made no attempt to curb it. He was tired of Sadamichi's jibes, and tired of pretending to be meek.

"I said you talk too much," he replied, "and my name is Jimmu."

Sadamichi squinted down his nose at Jimmu.

"You should say *sir* when you address someone of my standing," he said peevishly. "You obviously need a lesson in manners. I was brought up to respect my betters."

"So was I," said Jimmu.

The other guards swapped amazed looks. Jimmu was doing the prodding now.

Sadamichi smiled. "Am I intended to take that as an insult?"

"Take it any way you like," said Jimmu.

Sadamichi deftly rolled the chopstick between

the fingers of his right hand.

"You've a lot to learn, Farm Boy!" he said with a sigh. "I'll overlook your ignorance this once, but let me offer you a little advice. Don't offend a man unless you're as good a swordsman as he is."

"But I'm not as good a swordsman as you are, Sadamichi," said Jimmu. "I'm better."

Lightning pulsed through the opened shutters. A second later there was a peal of thunder.

"Perhaps you'd care to prove it, Farm Boy?" Sadamichi said. "We could go to the exercise yard and settle the matter with wooden practice-swords. Just a bout between friends. I wouldn't dream of challenging you to a proper duel, of course. It would be dishonourable of a man like me to kill a peasant."

"I'm not a peasant, and I'm not your friend," said Jimmu. "And I'm not afraid to fight you."

He felt giddy, and hardly recognized himself. Who was this headstrong youth disobeying all of Nichiren's instructions?

Rain rattled against the shingles on the roof.

"Good!" someone commented. "It'll clear the air."

He was not talking about the storm.

News of the duel spread quickly throughout the castle, so that by the time Jimmu and Sadamichi reached the exercise yard, quite a crowd had gathered. Bets were being exchanged, though few were laid in favour of Jimmu.

The storm was at its height. Rain fell in white lances; the thunder and the lightning came simultaneously. It was as dark as twilight.

The lightning illuminated the wet faces of the waiting men. Suddenly, they shuffled aside, and to Jimmu's surprise, Captain Muraki and Sergeant Hankei appeared.

Despite the rain, Jimmu and Sadamichi were bareheaded. They were removing their breastplates and armoured sleeves, but both snapped to attention as the captain approached.

"At ease," said Captain Muraki. "I've been told that there is bad feeling between the two of you. Is it true?"

"We've had a slight difference of opinion, sir," Sadamichi said smoothly.

"Sadamichi, to avoid this fight, would you be

prepared to apologize to Jimmu?" enquired Captain Muraki.

"I don't believe that I'm the one at fault, sir."

Captain Muraki turned to Jimmu, and said, "Will you apologize to Sadamichi?"

"No, sir," said Jimmu.

"Then I will act as referee," Captain Muraki said. "Select your weapons!"

The practice-swords were kept in a rack on one side of the yard. They were the same size and weight as real swords, but their blades were made from strips of wood bound together with cord.

After Jimmu and Sadamichi had chosen their swords, Captain Muraki briefly examined them to ensure that they were in good order.

"The contest will commence when I give the word," he said. "It will end when one of you lands a blow that would be fatal with a real sword. Stand ready!"

Jimmu and Sadamichi faced each other.

Jimmu held his sword in both hands. The base of the hilt rested against his right hip.

Sadamichi also employed the double-handed grip, but raised his sword above his head.

The captain called out, "Fight!"

To Jimmu, time slowed down. Drawing on everything that Nichiren had taught him, he focused his attention on Sadamichi until the man he faced was the only person in the world. Jimmu became a mirror that reflected every thought in Sadamichi's mind.

Sadamichi was smugly confident. He was certain that the boy must be quaking with fear. Jimmu's stance left his right side unguarded and vulnerable to attack. Sadamichi adjusted his position a fraction of a centimetre, to balance himself correctly, in a movement so slight as to be almost invisible.

But Jimmu saw it. He dropped onto one knee, rolled his wrists and swung his sword.

The wooden blade hit Sadamichi just below the ribcage, in the stroke known as "first body cut". Sadamichi stared blankly, unable to believe what had happened.

Men shouted and clapped their hands.

"Did you see that, sir?" Sergeant Hankei muttered to Captain Muraki. "The speed of the boy! Shall I order the men inside, sir?"

"No," said the captain. "The duel isn't over yet."

The captain was right. Sadamichi's vacant eyes filled with fury. His lips trembled; a flicker of lightning illuminated his ashen face.

"Witchcraft!" he cried. "You cast some sort of spell over me, Farm Boy! I demand you fight me again – with real swords!"

"As you wish," said Jimmu.

Thunder roared.

"Captain Muraki, this cannot be permitted!" protested Sergeant Hankei.

The captain did not look at Sergeant Hankei, but glanced towards the upper storey of the castle, where two shadowy figures watched from a half-opened shutter. One of the figures raised a hand, and the captain looked away.

"It will happen with or without my permission, sergeant," he said. "If they don't fight here today, they'll sneak off to fight another time."

"But one may kill the other, sir!"

"They are soldiers, sergeant," Captain Muraki said. "Facing death is part of their job."

Jimmu and Sadamichi had left their swords with their armour. They retrieved their weapons, unsheathed them, and squared up to each other.

Jimmu felt the familiar weight of his sword. It was his only inheritance from his father, and had been passed down through the Shimomura family for more than two hundred years. Jimmu had trained with it so often that it had become like an extension of his arm; the sharpness of its cutting edge matched the strength of his will.

Once again, the captain called out, "Stand ready!" then, "Fight!"

Once again, Jimmu concentrated. He had enraged Sadamichi, and angry men were liable to be careless.

He'll attack quickly, before he's properly ready, thought Jimmu.

And Sadamichi did.

Jimmu ducked, and Sadamichi's sword scythed over his head. He darted behind Sadamichi, who wheeled around. The swords rang as they clashed together, and squealed as they were drawn apart.

Jimmu pirouetted and pranced. Sadamichi slashed at Jimmu's legs. Jimmu hopped above the blade.

"The boy is playing with Sadamichi!" exclaimed Sergeant Hankei.

"The boy is making sure he stays alive," Captain Muraki replied.

Sadamichi's strokes were desperate and wild. He was taken in by a feint, and dropped his guard.

Jimmu's sword flashed in an arc.

All the watching men breathed in sharply. They expected to see a headless corpse collapse in a bloody welter.

But Jimmu stopped the apparent death-stroke. Instead of decapitating Sadamichi, the edge of his sword merely grazed his opponent's neck. Thin beads of red oozed out of his skin.

Sadamichi was defeated, outclassed, stunned and humiliated. He had never fought a swordsman as controlled as Jimmu, and he hung his head as he said, "You are the better swordsman. I apologize for insulting you."

"And I accept your apology," Jimmu said.

Sadamichi hurried off through the slackening rain.

"Sergeant Hankei, disperse the men," said Captain Muraki. "Jimmu, stay here. Someone wishes to speak with you."

Jimmu waited obediently, thinking, What does he

mean? Who wants to speak with me?

The storm had passed over. The thunder was no more than a faint growl, and the rain stopped as abruptly as it had begun.

A door opened; a man stepped through, and began to trudge across the exercise yard.

"Bow, Jimmu!" the captain whispered. "It's Lord Ankan himself!"

Jimmu bent his head and stared at his feet, forcing himself to breathe evenly. His pulse throbbed in his ears, but above the throbbing he heard the moist sound Lord Ankan's sandals made on the wet ground. He glimpsed the hem of a grey cotton kimono.

A hard, clipped voice said, "Is this the new recruit you told me about, captain?"

"Yes, My Lord, this is Guardsman Jimmu," responded Captain Muraki.

"Hmm!" grunted Lord Ankan. "Let me see your face, guardsman."

Jimmu steeled himself, and slowly raised his eyes. What he saw came as a profound shock.

Without his armour on, Choju Ankan did not look like an insect, or a demon. He was a middle-aged man of medium height and build, whose clothes were simple and sombre. His black hair was tied back in a pigtail with three pleats. His nose was straight, and his chin was firm beneath a grizzled beard. His gaze was shrewd and solemn. He keeps his evil hidden, thought Jimmu. It doesn't show in his eyes. He is good at deceiving people.

"You fought well, guardsman," said Lord Ankan. "Why didn't you kill Sadamichi while you had the chance?"

"I didn't consider his death to be necessary, My Lord," Jimmu said.

"Hmm!" said Lord Ankan. "You may live to regret your decision. Sadamichi is not the type of man who forgives and forgets. Captain Muraki tells me that your ambition is to become a samurai."

"Yes, My Lord."

"Then learn self-control!" Lord Ankan declared coldly. "A good samurai does not involve himself in petty squabbles. He saves his sword for the battlefield. That's all, guardsman. Carry on, Captain Muraki."

Lord Ankan turned abruptly, marched across the exercise yard and re-entered the castle.

Jimmu's shoulders sagged as it dawned upon him that at any point during their exchange, he could have drawn his sword and killed Lord Ankan.

Why didn't I? he wondered. What stopped me?

"Lord Ankan is right about Sadamichi, Jimmu," said Captain Muraki. "He'll try to get his own back one way or another. I'd watch your step, if I were you. You've made an enemy."

I have nothing but enemies, Jimmu told himself.

A sense of failure and a feeling of self-disgust rolled over him in a cold wave.

Chapter 6
Mistukage Castle
ISE PROVINCE, AUTUMN 1572

Summer turned into autumn. The weather cooled and the days shortened. The countryside around Mitsukage Castle resounded with the traditional songs of farm labourers gathering the harvest. Autumn also brought rumours. The castle was visited by a steady stream of messengers from Lord Nobunaga and Lord Tokugawa, who were allies of Lord Ankan. Veterans read the signs, and began to mutter that a campaign was in the offing.

One evening, as Jimmu was leaving the mess hall, he was hailed by Sergeant Hankei.

"Captain Muraki requires your presence in his quarters immediately," the sergeant said.

Jimmu saluted, and promptly obeyed the summons, but he felt uneasy. He had come to respect Captain Muraki's perceptive intelligence, almost to the point of fear. If anybody could find Jimmu out, it would be Ishida Muraki.

The captain was seated cross-legged on the dais in the long room, where he had first interviewed Jimmu. He was working at a writing desk, dashing down characters on a sheet of parchment. As soon as Jimmu entered, the captain set down his brush.

"In three days' time, Lady Takeko intends to travel to the shrine at Zato," he said. "Her grandmother is unwell, and Lady Takeko wishes to leave an offering, and pray for Lady Murasaki's recovery. You will accompany her as a member of her guard."

Jimmu bowed.

"To be frank, I consider this journey to be ill advised," the captain went on. "I have received reports that Takeda soldiers have been seen in the Zato area."

Jimmu was intrigued.

"But the Takeda family are enemies of Lord Ankan, because of his alliance with Lord Tokugawa and Lord Nobunaga, sir," he said.

Captain Muraki raised an eyebrow.

"I commend you for your knowledge," he said.

"One of my informants believes that the soldiers are disgraced samurai that Lord Takeda Shingen weeded out from his army. Maybe they're simply passing through Lord Ankan's territory, maybe they're planning a daring raid to try and win back Lord Shingen's favour. However it may be, I am anxious about this journey of Lady Takeko's."

Jimmu thought that the solution was simple.

"Wouldn't it be better if Lady Takeko postponed her visit until after the Takeda men have been dealt with, sir?" he said.

The effect of this question was remarkable. Captain Muraki rocked with laughter, and slapped his palms against his thighs. It took him almost a minute to regain his composure.

"Forgive me, Jimmu, but you don't know Lady Takeko," he said, his voice husky from laughing. "She has a fearsome temper, and once her mind is set upon something, no one can persuade her otherwise. Her mother died shortly after she was born, and Lord Ankan was so stricken with grief that he vowed never to marry again. The memory of his wife has made him overindulgent towards his daughter. Lady Takeko is used to getting her own way. She is wilful, and speaks her mind directly. This mission may be important for your career, Jimmu. Lord Ankan gave specific orders that you were to be one of Lady Takeko's guards."

"I am deeply honoured, sir," said Jimmu.

The situation was almost amusing. Jimmu had vowed to avenge his father by taking Choju Ankan's life – now Lord Ankan had chosen Jimmu to protect his daughter. Though the irony was not lost on Jimmu, he quickly forgot about it. The prospect of seeing Lady Takeko again dominated his thoughts.

That evening, Jimmu was surprised when Sadamichi sat next to him in the mess hall. Since their sword fight, Sadamichi had done his best to avoid Jimmu, but now he greeted him like an old friend, and joked with him while they ate.

Jimmu's suspicions were aroused. Sadamichi's oily charm did not affect him. The man's smile seemed warm enough, but his eyes remained cold and sly.

After the meal was finished, Sadamichi followed Jimmu outside. Above the castle walls, the sky was darkening, and showing a scattering of pale stars.

"Have you heard the latest?" Sadamichi enquired casually. "They say that Lord Ankan's brat has nagged him into letting her visit some shrine or other."

Jimmu became defensive.

"I don't listen to gossip," he said.

"Are you sure you haven't heard anything?" said Sadamichi.

"What Lady Takeko does is none of my business, or yours!" Jimmu snapped.

Sadamichi laughed a little too loudly.

"No need to take offence," he said. "I was just asking. I like to gather information that might be useful."

"Useful to whom?"

"To whoever might be interested," said Sadamichi.

"I must go now," Jimmu said. "Captain Muraki wishes me to report to him."

"Give the captain my best regards," Sadamichi said, as Jimmu turned away with a sense of unease and suspicion. Why was Sadamichi suddenly being so friendly?

✦

Three days later at sunup, two bearers carried a covered litter, with sliding doors, into the main courtyard. Here they were joined by Jimmu and three other guards, all armed with spears and swords.

Lady Takeko, dressed in a white silk kimono and a wide-brimmed hat with a veil so thick that it completely obscured her face, came out of the castle, accompanied by Lord Ankan. Before Lady Takeko stepped into the litter, Lord Ankan presented her with a small wooden box.

Jimmu did not catch the words Lord Ankan spoke to his daughter, but the tender tone in which they were spoken surprised him, as did the soft expression on His Lordship's face.

The travelling party crossed the bridge over the moat, passed through the outer gates of Mitsukage Castle, and set off at a brisk pace along the road that led to the shrine at Zato.

Dawn had drawn down a mist as thick and grey as old cobwebs. Sounds were muffled. Other travellers on the road appeared as solid shadows.

In the quiet place inside him, Jimmu's thoughts

wandered. Choju Ankan had behaved unexpectedly. Nichiren had depicted the man as monstrously selfish, but there had been genuine concern in his eyes when he parted from his daughter. Jimmu could not help but compare this with the fragmentary memories he had of his own parents. They had always seemed distant to him, his mother as beautiful and remote as a goddess, his father stiff and formal. Neither of them had ever treated him with the gentleness Ankan had shown Lady Takeko.

Still, Jimmu remarked cynically to himself, even devils are kind to their own.

After two hours of travelling, the party stopped by the side of the road so that the litter bearers could rest. The mist had lifted a little. Trees had trunks and branches, but no tops.

As Jimmu sat on a boulder, a guard named Kanji approached him. Ever since the duel with Sadamichi, Kanji had gone out of his way to be friendly to Jimmu. He was one of the few who had wagered on the youngster's success, and his winnings had made him kindly disposed. Kanji had a slightly pudgy face, with bright eyes, and loved drinking, gambling and good company. He leaned his weight against his spear and yawned.

"Not much further now," he said. "The shrine's less than an hour's march from here." He lowered his voice. "At least the brat's been quiet, which is something to be grateful for. I've heard that she's pretty. I haven't seen her myself, but I wouldn't mind. There's no harm in looking, you know?"

"No, I don't know," said Jimmu.

Kanji shook his head.

"You're an odd one, Jimmu," he said. "None of the guards knows what to make of you."

"I want to be a samurai," said Jimmu.

"Personally, my ambition is to die of old age," Kanji said with a laugh.

"I'll die young," said Jimmu.

Kanji appeared taken aback.

"You sound very positive of that," he said.

"It's my destiny," said Jimmu. "Destiny can't be avoided."

The words were Nichiren's; the destiny belonged

to Jimmu. He would sacrifice his life to regain his father's honour.

"When you have slain Lord Ankan, you can embrace death with joy in your heart," Nichirin had said. "Your purpose in life will be fulfilled. To die honourably is better than living in shame."

The shrine was on the side of a hill wooded with pine trees that scented the air. It was a humble place, just three black rocks that vaguely resembled seated figures. Offerings had been left around the feet of the rocks — bowls of rice, cups of wine, withered bundles of summer flowers.

The bearers set down the litter, and one of them tapped at the doors. Lady Takeko emerged, holding the box that her father had presented to her. She walked slowly to the rocks, placed the box on the ground, and lowered her head in prayer.

The guards and the bearers relaxed. They drank water from their canteens and broke out their rations: rice balls and cold bean stew.

Jimmu did not join them. He stood watching Lady

Takeko. She remained completely motionless, and Jimmu admired her powers of self-control and concentration.

The men finished eating, and sat round in a circle. Kanji produced a pair of dice.

"Hey, Jimmu!" he called. "Fancy a game of chance?"

"I don't gamble," said Jimmu.

"Then you're wiser than Sadamichi," Kanji said laughing. "He was up till all hours last night, dicing in the mess hall. I don't know where his money came from, but I know where a lot of it went, because I won it from him."

The men chuckled mockingly, then settled to their game.

Jimmu frowned and looked around. The lower slopes of the hill were clear, and there was no one on the road. Uphill there was nothing to be seen but the last of the mists clinging to the trees, yet Jimmu felt that something was wrong. The atmosphere of the shrine was more tense than tranquil.

Jimmu screened out the voices of the gambling men, and listened intently. A startled bird chattered;

the wind hissed through the branches of the pines; a horse snorted, and then, somewhere close by, metal chinked softly on metal.

"Ambush!" Jimmu yelled.

The men in the circle turned, startled, and hesitated for a split second. An arrow pierced the left eye of the guard seated next to Kanji, killing him instantly. The circle broke in panic.

Between the misty trees, six riders galloped downhill towards the shrine. They were all armed.

Chapter 7
Zato

ISE PROVINCE, AUTUMN 1572

Just as when he fought the duel with Sadamichi, Jimmu entered a different kind of time. Seconds slowed down and stretched out, allowing him to take in tiny details: the snarling mouth and yellow teeth of the leading samurai; the diamond-shaped leaf badge of the Takeda clan on the crest of his helmet; the brown pine needles kicked up by the hoofs of his horse. Jimmu saw a second arrow flick through the air like the blink of a shadow, and he heard the scream of the litter bearer that the arrow took down.

Lady Takeko began to get to her feet.

"Stay low!" barked Jimmu.

He lowered his spear and advanced. The leading samurai was almost on top of him. The man held a long sword at arm's length. His eyes bulged.

Jimmu braced the spear against his side, ignored

the bulk of the horse bearing down on him, and concentrated his attention on its rider.

Before the samurai could use his sword, he rode onto the point of Jimmu's spear. Momentum drove the blade of the spear in through his breastplate and out through his back. He tumbled from the saddle, wrenching the shaft of the spear from Jimmu's hands. The horse galloped on, riderless.

Jimmu turned his head and felt a faint draught, as an arrow hummed past his right ear. The archer was riding at him, already bending his bow and firing again.

Time slowed down even further. Jimmu saw the arrow flying towards him, the head seeming to swell as it approached, the flight feathers ruffling. Jimmu drew his sword and with an instinctive twitch of his wrist, deflected the arrow with the blade, brought the weapon round to slash the archer across the chest, then twisted it to slash him across the back as he rode by.

The archer fell. His foot caught in a stirrup, and the horse dragged its dead master along behind it.

There was a shrill scream. A rider had dismounted

at the shrine, and was struggling with Lady Takeko. Her pale arms beat at him, like the flapping wings of a swan. She kicked and cursed. Her hat and veil had been torn off.

Jimmu rushed to her aid.

The samurai caught sight of him and pushed Lady Takeko to the ground. He reached for his sword, but never drew it.

Using all his strength, Jimmu brought down his sword in a stroke called "priest's robe". The edge of the blade sliced diagonally through the samurai's right collarbone, severing his head, neck, left arm and shoulder from the rest of his body.

Blood sprayed Jimmu's face. Without bothering to wipe it away, he wheeled around to locate the other riders.

Both the litter bearers were dead, and apart from Jimmu, the only guard still alive was Kanji. He had killed one rider, and was now under attack from the remaining two. They held their horses on shortened reins as they tried to hack at him. Kanji held a spear in each hand and kept the samurai at bay, lunging and parrying with great skill.

As Jimmu hurried over to him, Kanji killed the rider on his left with a jab to his throat, but the other rider felled him with a swordstroke.

There was no time for the rider to alter position and defend himself against Jimmu. Jimmu took off the man's left leg just below the knee, hauled him out of the saddle and finished him with a two-handed thrust that sent the sword through the samurai's breastbone.

Jimmu kneeled beside his fallen companion.

Kanji, not quite dead, was trembling violently. He wanted to speak, but all that passed his chattering teeth was, "Be...be..." Then his trembling ceased and his eyes glazed over.

Jimmu knew what Kanji had been trying to say.

"Betrayed!" he whispered to himself. "We were betrayed by someone at Mitsukage Castle."

A shadow fell across Kanji's corpse. Jimmu sprang to his feet, ready to fight, but the shadow had been cast by Lady Takeko, not an enemy. She stared at him in horrified wonder, while the breeze blew strands of her long, fine hair across her face. The white silk of her kimono was speckled red with blood.

Jimmu was lost. Lady Takeko's presence wiped away the rest of the world.

"You fought courageously," she said.

Jimmu bobbed his head to acknowledge the compliment.

"We must find somewhere for you to hide, My Lady," he said. "Once you're safe, I'll go back to the castle for help."

"No you won't!" said Lady Takeko. "You'll round up a couple of horses and we'll ride back together. I'm not staying here alone."

"But, My Lady!" Jimmu protested. "There may be other Takeda samurai nearby. You'll draw more attention to yourself on horseback."

Lady Takeko glared.

"I already have the attention of the entire Takeda family," she said. "Lord Shingen wants to kidnap me, marry me off to one of his cronies and force my father into an alliance. Stop wasting time and find those horses. And stop calling me *My Lady*. When we're at the castle you can fawn and grovel all you please. Out here, it turns my stomach. My name is Takeko. I graciously give you permission to use it – just this once."

Only one of the riders' horses was anywhere to be seen. Jimmu caught hold of its reins, and the animal placidly followed him.

Takeko petted the horse's neck and made clicking noises with her tongue. The horse swivelled its ears to listen, and whinnied softly.

Takeko took hold of the saddle and slipped her foot into a stirrup. When Jimmu made as if to lift her, she stopped him with a disdainful look and swung herself up with apparent ease.

"I've been getting on and off horses by myself since I was eight years old," she said.

"I'm sorry, My – I mean – I'm sorry!" said Jimmu. "You ride, I'll walk."

Takeko laughed scornfully.

"Don't be stupid!" she said. "Get on behind me. There's just about room for the two of us."

Jimmu climbed into the saddle and squeezed in behind Takeko, his face hot and red with embarrassment.

Takeko kicked her heels and urged the horse into a canter.

"Who taught you how to fight like that?" she demanded brusquely.

Nichiren's face flashed into Jimmu's mind.

"An old man," he said.

"Your grandfather?"

"No, only an old man I used to know. He died last spring."

Takeko sighed in exasperation.

"The oldest person I know is my grandmother," she said. "She's so old-fashioned that it drives me mad. She pesters me about being polite, and meek. She says I must learn to flirt properly so that I can marry a rich husband. Hah!"

Jimmu smelled the perfume in Takeko's hair.

"Would marrying a rich man be so bad?" he asked.

"You don't understand, because you're male," replied Takeko. "You can have adventures and go to war. Women are supposed to look pretty, have babies and arrange flowers. Men have choices."

"Not all men," Jimmu said.

Takeko twisted around in the saddle to peer at him. "Why do you look so sad?" she said. "You're the saddest-looking boy I've ever seen."

Jimmu countered with a question of his own.

"Is that what made you talk to me instead of calling the guards that night in the private quarters?" he said.

"No!"

"Then why did you talk to me?"

"It isn't any of your business!" said Takeko.

Her icy tone put Jimmu into a silence that lasted all the way back to Mitsukage Castle.

Jimmu and Takeko reached the castle late in the afternoon, the dipping sun casting long shadows in front of them. Before they came in sight of the castle, Jimmu had insisted on dismounting, and leading the horse by its bridle, saying that it would be disrespectful for him to be seen sharing a mount with Lord Ankan's daughter. They passed through the castle's outer gates and crossed the bridge over the moat, the horse's hoofs clattering on the wooden boards.

As they waited for the main gate to be opened, Jimmu glanced upwards and saw a startled face gazing at him from the gatehouse – it was Sadamichi.

Jimmu instantly recalled what Kanji had told him

about the money Sadamichi had lost gambling, and remembered how curious Sadamichi had been about Takeko's comings and goings.

It was Sadamichi! He's the one who betrayed us to the Takeda, thought Jimmu.

As soon as the gate had opened wide enough, Jimmu slipped inside the castle. Silently he unsheathed his sword and began the ascent up to the gatehouse where Sadamichi was waiting.

Chapter 8
Mistukage Castle
ISE PROVINCE, AUTUMN 1572

On his way up the stairs to the gatehouse, Jimmu set aside his outrage at what Sadamichi had done. Instead, he focused on the revulsion he felt, so that his mind would stay clear and cool.

Another guard, who was on duty with Sadamichi, scowled when Jimmu entered the room.

"What d'you mean by busting in here with a drawn sword?" he snapped.

"Stay out of this," Jimmu warned, fixing his gaze on Sadamichi.

Sadamichi's face was grey with fear. His lips writhed into a false smile.

"Eh, Jimmu!" he blustered. "Was that you I saw with Lady Takeko just now? Where's the rest of the party?"

Jimmu was not deceived by Sadamichi's show of cheeriness.

"How long have you been taking money from the Takeda?" he asked quietly. "What price did they pay for the information about Lady Takeko's visit to Zato – five pieces of gold? Ten?"

"What money?" demanded Sadamichi. He turned to the other guard. "I haven't got a clue what he's raving about. Me, a spy in the pay of the Takeda? Did you ever hear such rubbish? The boy must be drunk, or crazy!"

Jimmu noticed Sadamichi's right hand creep a fraction nearer to the sword at his waist.

"What was their plan – to capture Lady Takeko and then kill the guards to leave no witnesses?" Jimmu said. "You've acted dishonourably, Sadamichi. You betrayed your comrades to the enemy."

Sadamichi could tell that there was no further point in lying to Jimmu, but if he could distract the boy, he might be able to kill him, and then make his escape.

"Who the enemy is depends on your point of view!" he snorted. "There are grander castles than Mitsukage, and greater lords than Lord Ankan. Those men who died were no comrades of mine. Ignorant peasants, the lot of them. They got exactly what they deserved, and now it's your turn, Farm Boy!"

Sadamichi seized his sword from its scabbard.

Jimmu's sword sighed as he swung it horizontally, then flicked it upwards through the flesh, bones and sinews of Sadamichi's right wrist. The severed hand fell to the floorboards, where it lay like a pale crab.

Sadamichi squealed, and clutched the bloody stump where his right hand had been.

"Quickly! Tie a cord around his arm to stop the bleeding," Jimmu told the other guard. "Sadamichi, I'm taking you straight to Captain Muraki."

"Why bother?" croaked Sadamichi. "Finish me here, and let me be done with it."

Jimmu narrowed his eyes.

"Death by the sword is too good for a traitor," he said. "When you've made your confession to the captain, he'll have you hung as a common criminal."

Late that night, hours after Sadamichi had been questioned, sentenced and executed, Jimmu was called to Captain Muraki's quarters.

Jimmu saluted, sat down, then waited while the captain subjected him to a long searching look.

"You did well for yourself today, Jimmu," Captain Muraki said, at last.

"I did my duty, sir," replied Jimmu.

"You did far better than that, and you know it. Lord Ankan will be grateful to you for rescuing his daughter." A strange smile spread across Captain Muraki's mouth. "But that was your intention, wasn't it?"

"Sir?"

"I know what your plans are, Jimmu."

Jimmu felt as if the floor had been pulled out from under him, leaving him falling through black nothing. His mind churned. Could he bluff his way out, or would he have to kill the captain? If he did, how far would he get before the castle's guards captured him? A coppery taste filled his mouth.

"You are a guardsman, but you have higher ambitions," the captain continued. "You had faith in yourself. You gambled that one day there would come a chance to use your skills in a way that would impress an important lord – such as Lord Ankan. Today you got that chance, and you seized it. What are you hoping for, Jimmu – money, land?"

Relief surged from the nape of Jimmu's neck to

the base of his spine; the captain had not discovered his secret.

"I hope to be promoted, sir, so I'll have an opportunity to better myself," he said.

"Ah yes! Your desire to be a samurai," said the captain. "More than one person has mentioned your talking about it. Did you mean what you said?"

"Of course!"

The captain pursed his lips.

"But are you ready yet?" he wondered aloud. "The old monk who trained you at Sengen monastery—"

"Soun," Jimmu said promptly.

"He taught you how to fight, but fighting does not make you a warrior," said the captain. "The way of the samurai is difficult, but it's also pure and noble. Every day, a samurai must battle with himself to attain perfection, knowing that he will fall short. Every night, he must rest in order to renew the struggle the following morning. Above all else, a samurai must learn to be obedient. His first duty is unquestioning devotion to his lord, to the point where he will willingly give up his life if it is required of him."

Jimmu was puzzled. The only devotion Nichiren

had mentioned was devotion to the memory of Jimmu's father.

The captain became awkward. He shifted his haunches, cleared his throat, scratched his chin.

"This brings me to a delicate matter," he said. "Earlier this evening, I was granted the honour of an audience with Lady Takeko. She talked incessantly about your courage, strength and gallantry."

Jimmu lowered his face to conceal a blush.

"Lady Takeko is almost sixteen," said Captain Muraki. "Sometimes she behaves like a child, and sometimes like a grown woman. Such girls are impressionable, and liable to form attachments that are unsuitable. Are you listening to me, Jimmu?"

Jimmu raised his head. "Yes, sir!"

"If Lady Takeko should seek out your company again in future, you are to discourage her," the captain said. "You will remind her that she is your mistress, and you are her servant."

"Sir?" said Jimmu, far from certain of the captain's meaning.

"Let this be a test of your obedience," the captain declared. "If you fail, you risk undoing everything that you achieved today. I foresee a danger Lady Takeko may become too fond of you. Do all that you can to prevent this from happening, or you will earn Lord Ankan's wrath as quickly as you earned his gratitude. It is not acceptable for young ladies to have tender feelings towards guardsmen. That is all I have to say for the present, Jimmu. Leave me."

Outside, in the chilly air of the courtyard, Jimmu was not sure whether he had been praised or chided, and he was confused by his reaction to Captain Muraki's warning. The possibility that Takeko might be fond of him was oddly appealing. But his mood swiftly changed from confusion to resentment.

Discourage Lady Takeko? he thought, as he trudged towards the barracks. Why would I want to have anything more to do with her? She's vain, rude and argumentative. She may look beautiful, but beauty means nothing. Beauty doesn't last. Determination and dedication, those are the vital things!

As he passed the exercise yard, Jimmu heard an irritating creaking noise that caused him to turn his head.

Torches were burning around the yard, illuminating the body of Sadamichi, dangling from a makeshift gibbet. The gibbet's wooden joints creaked as the corpse swayed slowly in the wind.

I don't want to die like that, thought Jimmu. I don't want to die in shame, but in glory, with my sword in my hand, and Choju Ankan's body stretched out in front of me.

A sudden doubt stopped him in mid-stride. Captain Muraki had told him that a samurai's first duty was obedience to his lord — but surely that meant that a samurai had to be certain that a lord was worthy of his obedience. How had Lord Ankan convinced an honest man like Captain Muraki to serve him? Would the captain really be willing to sacrifice himself in order to protect a scheming coward?

Before coming to Mitsukage Castle, Jimmu had thought he knew the truth about Lord Ankan, but the longer he stayed, the more shadowy the truth seemed. And what of his own truth? He had fancied that Nichiren trained him to be a samurai, but increasingly it seemed that all Nichiren had taught him was how to use samurai weapons. It appeared there was more to being a samurai than simply killing.

"You will die a hero's death," Nichiren had maintained: but how could an assassin be a hero?

Jimmu's ruthless determination was beginning to waver.

Chapter 9
Mistukage Castle
ISE PROVINCE, AUTUMN 1572

Four days later, Jimmu served his first turn at night duty, standing watch on the battlements of the outer wall. He was accompanied by Kambei, a veteran soldier with a seamed scar on one cheek, and two fingers missing from his left hand. Between patrols, he and Jimmu warmed themselves at a charcoal brazier, and Jimmu listened while Kambei told tales about the campaigns he had taken part in. His comments gave Jimmu an entirely different view of the power struggle between the warring lords.

"Takeda Shingen is the commander to watch out for," Kambei declared at one point. "He's as cunning as a rat. His battle banner reads, *Swift as the Wind, Calm as the Forest, Fierce as the Wildfire, Steady as the Mountain*, and that's the way he likes to fight. The great opponent of the Takeda family is Lord Oda

Nobunaga. He's a cruel and ruthless warrior who is determined to rule over all of Japan. Lord Nobunaga's most loyal ally is Lord Tokugawa Ieyasu. Many nobles look down on Lord Ieyasu because he comes from a peasant family, and started his career as a common soldier, but he's a brave fighter and a gifted commander."

"What kind of commander is Lord Ankan?" enquired Jimmu.

"You'll find out for yourself soon enough," Kambei assured him. "The Takeda are on the move. They've laid siege to Futamata Castle. If it falls, Lord Ieyasu will ask Lord Nobunaga for help, and Lord Nobunaga will send for Lord Ankan."

The prospect of battle thrilled Jimmu.

"Are battlefields as glorious as they say?" he asked eagerly.

Kambei looked at him askance.

"Glory is all in the mind of storytellers, lad," he said grimly. "Battlefields are crazy places. All you see of a battle is your little bit of it. No one really knows what's going on, and you're generally too busy surviving to bother trying to make sense of anything.

Let me give you a piece of advice. When you go into battle keep your head down and do as you're told."

"But what about single combat, and the noble sacrifice of samurai?" said Jimmu, repeating a few phrases that Nichiren had drilled into him.

"Noble sacrifices are all very well in stories, but they don't win battles," Kambei said.

Before Jimmu could ask Kambei to explain further, the sound of a footstep made him wheel around, and lower his spear.

"Who's there?" he challenged.

A maidservant came out of the dark, into the glow of the brazier. She wore a pale silk kimono. Her hair was elaborately pinned up, and her face was white with make-up. The wooden blocks on the soles and heels of her sandals forced her to take tiny, mincing steps. She bowed to Jimmu.

"I must talk with you," she said.

"Talk to me about what?" said Jimmu, mystified.

"A private matter."

Kambei grunted.

"I know when to make myself scarce!" he said to Jimmu. "If you need me, I'll be down by the gatehouse."

When Kambei was out of earshot, the maidservant said, "Lady Takeko wishes to see you. She is waiting by the pool in the garden near the archery hall."

"But I can't leave my post!" retorted Jimmu.

The maidservant's shoulders sagged.

"Then My Lady will be vexed, and she will take her anger out on me," she said.

Jimmu thought for a moment before saying, "All right. Tell Lady Takeko that I'll come."

The maidservant melted back into the night, and Jimmu went to find Kambei.

"What did that pretty girl want?" Kambei said, with a knowing wink.

Jimmu pretended to be embarrassed.

"Um, could you do me a favour, Kambei?" he said. "Can you manage on your own for a while? I have some, er, important business to attend to."

Kambei threw a mock punch at Jimmu's shoulder.

"Go on then, you young dog!" he chuckled. "And I'd leave your spear with me, if I were you. I don't think you'll be needing it."

Jimmu had thought long and hard about his conversation with Captain Muraki. It was clear now that the captain had been warning him that further contact with Lady Takeko might lead to his dismissal from the castle, which would ruin his plans. This present summons would provide him with the perfect opportunity to point out the difference in their social standing, and shame Lady Takeko into leaving him alone. All the same, by meeting her, he knew he was going against the captain's advice.

The garden near the archery hall was lit by moonlight. Ornamental boulders appeared silvery, evergreen trees and shrubs were grey. Takeko was standing at the edge of a pool that was spanned by a delicate bridge. She was holding a scarlet shawl around the shoulders of her white shift.

As Jimmu drew near, Takeko turned and gazed at him. Jimmu felt as if someone had struck him in the stomach. Takeko was far lovelier than he remembered, so lovely that he almost forgot what he had intended to say. With an effort, he pulled himself together and bowed formally.

"You sent for me, My Lady?" he said.

"Yes," Takeko replied haughtily. "I'm bored, and I thought that talking to you might distract me." Her manner suddenly changed, and she sighed. "The truth is, I'm lonely," she confessed. "Most of my maids are older than I am, and those that aren't are stupid. All they do is giggle, and talk about lip-paint and boys."

Jimmu knew that he ought to protest about being dragged away from guard duty simply in order to chat, but all he could think to say was, "And lip-paint and boys don't interest you?"

"I'm terrified that they might one day," Takeko said with a shudder. "Imagine a life small enough for such things to seem important! At Zato, it was exciting. There were arrows, and shouting, and blood, and death."

"You want me to kill somebody for your entertainment?" said Jimmu.

"No!" exclaimed Takeko. "It's just that when you were fighting, you looked as if you were doing what you were born to do, and I envied you. I don't know what I was born to do. I probably never will."

Though he could not account for it, Jimmu sensed a kind of danger in the sadness of Takeko's voice, and the moonlight shining on her neck. He longed to hear her laugh, but he quelled the longing and said, "I've been ordered to stay away from you."

Takeko's eyes widened. "By whom?"

"Captain Muraki. He hinted that Lord Ankan would be displeased if he knew that his daughter was keeping company with a common guardsman."

"Captain Muraki is a numbskull!" hissed Takeko.

"He is concerned for your reputation."

"And what concerns you, Jimmu?"

"I don't want to be ordered to leave the castle," Jimmu said.

"It's not my father's displeasure that should worry you, it's mine!" Takeko said angrily. "One word from me, and you could lose more than your job. I could have you blinded, or boiled alive, or have your tongue torn out with white-hot pincers!"

Now she sounds like Choju Ankan's daughter! Jimmu thought.

Takeko's fit of pique exhausted itself, and she shook her head.

"I'm sorry, Jimmu," she said. "I'd never do any of those things. Why did you come here tonight?"

"Because you sent for me, My Lady," said Jimmu, "and because I felt it was my duty to tell you about Captain Muraki's orders."

Takeko turned away.

"If I send for you again, only come because you want to," she said, and she walked across the garden, towards the private quarters of the castle.

Jimmu remained at the pool, staring at the reflection of the moon on the water. The moon's tranquillity mocked his chaotic feelings. He was thrilled to have been with Takeko, and already longed for their next meeting: yet she was the daughter of Choju Ankan.

Stop this! Jimmu told himself. She is as much your enemy as her father is.

But the more he thought about Takeko, the harder it was to see her that way.

Chapter 10

Mistukage Castle

ISE PROVINCE, AUTUMN 1572

The following morning there was a cold snap. The puddles of autumn rain that filled the ruts in the road outside the castle whitened into cat ice; mud froze as hard as stone. The tiles on the roofs of the castle sparkled with frost. Off-duty men hung about the bathhouse and kitchens to keep warm.

Jimmu was so deep in thought that he barely registered the cold. He had told Lady Takeko what he believed it was his duty to say, but it was now obvious to him that his feelings towards her went beyond duty. Despite his best efforts to concentrate on his mission to kill Lord Ankan, daydreams flicked through his mind, like leaping grasshoppers. He imagined Takeko smiling at him, walking beside him along an avenue lined with blossoming cherry trees, laughing with him as they took cover from a sudden downpour...

The memory of Nichiren's voice broke through the dream.

"Your resolve has weakened!" Nichiren rasped. "You should not allow yourself to indulge in these emotions!"

But what are these emotions? Jimmu wondered.

That afternoon, in the bustling, noisy mess hall, Jimmu was still brooding, and did not notice when Kambei sat down opposite him.

Kambei glanced at Jimmu, and then at Jimmu's bowl, which was half filled with noodles, bean curd and seaweed.

"Are you leaving that, Jimmu?" Kambei said.

Jimmu blinked rapidly.

"Take it if you want," he said. "I'm not hungry."

Kambei emptied the contents of Jimmu's bowl into his own.

"Off your grub because you had a row with that pretty maid of yours?" he teased. "It must be love."

"Love?" gasped Jimmu.

"No need to be bashful, Jimmu," Kambei said.

"Believe it or not, I was your age once, and I had many lady friends."

Nostalgia made Kambei's eyes distant.

"Women!" he said with a sigh. "They're miraculous beings who bring new life into the world. They're goddesses who can transform a hovel into a paradise. I've never understood them."

Kambei's expression changed.

"Watch out, here's Captain Muraki!" he muttered. "Wonder who he's after?"

The answer was quick in coming. Captain Muraki saluted Jimmu, and said, "On your feet, guardsman. Lord Ankan has sent for you."

Jimmu stood up, and followed the captain across the hall. The little food he had eaten turned sour in his stomach. He breathed in deeply to steady his nerves. Lord Ankan must have found out about his liaison with Takeko, and was summoning the lowly guardsman to punish him. Had Takeko betrayed him? It did not matter. Nothing mattered now.

At the door of the mess hall, Jimmu reached out to take down his helmet from a peg.

"No, Jimmu," said Captain Muraki. "Leave your

helmet and spear where they are. Only bodyguards are permitted to carry weapons in His Lordship's presence."

It's of no importance, Jimmu said to himself. You know of seven ways to kill a man with your bare hands. Choju Ankan will die today, and you will die along with him.

Lord Ankan received Jimmu and Captain Muraki in a room that was far smaller and plainer than Jimmu had expected. A samurai stood guard outside, and two more were positioned in the room's far corners. Their presence, and the presence of Captain Muraki greatly decreased the chances of Jimmu making a successful attack.

Lord Ankan was seated on the floor, with his back to Jimmu and the captain. He was working on a painting. A sheet of paper had been spread out on a rush mat. Beside the mat were a bowl of water and an ink block. Ankan had sketched a mountain peak rising from a wooded valley, with three cranes flying across the sky. He worked quickly, his brush describing a curve here, a straight line there.

"Guardsman Jimmu, My Lord!" announced Captain Muraki.

Without breaking off from his painting, Lord Ankan said, "Have you ever painted, guardsman?"

"No, My Lord," replied Jimmu.

"I find it soothing," Lord Ankan said. "The marks on the paper draw me into other worlds. If my life had been different, I think that I might have been a painter."

His voice was stiff, as if he felt awkward at making this personal revelation.

"No man can escape his destiny, My Lord," said Jimmu.

Lord Ankan turned his head to give Jimmu a searching look.

"Many believe their lives are stories that have already been written, and so can't be changed," he said. "But it sometimes seems to me that we write our own stories, and decide our own destinies."

Jimmu could not decide whether these words were wise, or the delusions of a power-crazed tyrant who believed that he could control the course of history.

"The last time we met, you spoke of your desire to be a samurai," Lord Ankan said. "Is that still your wish?"

"Yes, My Lord."

"We'll see," said Lord Ankan. "I'm promoting you out of the guard. You'll serve as a trainee bodyguard. Captain Muraki will supervise your training. After you leave me, you will go with him to the archery hall. Your things will be brought to your new accommodation in the private quarters."

Jimmu felt frustrated. If he attempted to kill Lord Ankan, he would be cut down by the samurai. There was no point in wasting his life making an attack that was doomed to fail.

He bowed. "Yes, My Lord. Thank you, My Lord."

Jimmu turned to go. To his surprise, his frustration at failing to kill Lord Ankan was mixed with relief at still being alive, and he felt strangely proud of his promotion.

In the private quarters, you will be closer to Lord Ankan, he thought. You will have more opportunities to kill him.

"Jimmu?" Lord Ankan said.

"My Lord?" said Jimmu, turning back.

"Thank you for saving my daughter from my enemies."

Jimmu did not know what answer to make, and bowed again.

As he walked with Captain Muraki through the private quarters, Jimmu recalled a summer's day when, as a sulky thirteen year old, he had rebelled against his training, complaining that it was too difficult.

Instead of beating Jimmu, as he would normally have done, Nichiren punished him with words.

"You have spoken childishly, boy," he said. "You have no idea how fortunate you are. Most people lead lives that have no direction or meaning. You have a purpose, you know why you are on this earth, and what you have to do. Keep to that purpose. Without it, you are nothing but a traitor's son and an outcast."

Jimmu overcame his sense of failure. Today had not been his day to kill Lord Ankan, but the day would come.

"Patience," Nichiren's memory advised. "Fate will

show you the right time and place. When Choju Ankan least expects it, when he is at the height of victory, or in the depths of despair, you will offer him up to death."

Chapter 11
Mistukage Castle
ISE PROVINCE, AUTUMN 1572

The archery hall was long and narrow, with a high ceiling supported by two rows of wooden columns. At one end of the hall, small round targets stood in front of bales of straw that had been positioned to catch any stray shots. At the opposite end was a low platform with a rack of bows and a smaller rack of arrows. The afternoon light was already fading, and shadows thickened in the corners of the hall.

Captain Muraki and Jimmu seated themselves on the platform, and Captain Muraki smiled.

"You are a very fortunate young man, Jimmu," he said. "I congratulate you on your success."

"Thank you, sir," said Jimmu, thinking that it was skill and not good fortune that had brought him success.

The captain's smile vanished.

"I've seen for myself what kind of swordsman you are, and your spear work is excellent, but you are an incompetent archer," he said. "Why is that?"

The directness of the question took Jimmu by surprise.

"I – I don't know, sir," he said. "I'm just better with a sword than I am with a bow."

Captain Muraki showed his disapproval by hissing air through his teeth.

"Your previous teacher was negligent!" he exclaimed. "A samurai must be a master of all weapons. Archery is your weak spot. Very well. From now on you will dedicate yourself to overcoming that weakness. String a bow, and let's begin."

Jimmu selected a bow and prepared to fire it, painfully aware of the captain's watchful eyes.

The first shot flew wide to the left of Jimmu's chosen target.

"Again!" the captain rasped.

The second shot glanced off the target's edge.

Captain Muraki made no criticism, nor did he offer any helpful suggestions.

"Again!" he commanded.

And again, and again, and again, until Jimmu's arms and shoulders were sore, and the hall was gloomy with dusk.

"That last shot was your worst effort yet!" the captain scolded. "What's the matter with you?"

"It's almost dark," complained Jimmu. "How can I take aim at a target that I can hardly see?"

"Seeing has nothing to do with it," Captain Muraki announced. "Pass me the bow and I'll demonstrate."

The captain took three arrows from the rack and placed them beside him. For a moment he sat perfectly still with the bow resting across his lap, then he loosed off the arrows in rapid succession.

"I fired at the target on the far right," he told Jimmu. "Go and see."

Jimmu stood up and walked the length of the hall.

Captain Muraki's arrows were clustered tightly in the exact centre of the target.

Jimmu was awestruck.

"How did you do that, sir?" he asked.

"Answer me this first," said the captain. "When you had the bow, what were you trying to do?"

"To hit the target."

"Sloppy thinking!" said Captain Muraki. "A samurai should aim his arrow at the centre of himself. He must wait until his inner world is at one with the outer world, and then his centre and the target will coincide. He'll be able to hit it on foot, on the back of a galloping horse, or in the darkness. Think, Jimmu! Find your centre."

The captain put down the bow.

"That's enough for today," he said. "Meet me here at sunrise tomorrow."

Jimmu frowned deeply as he left the archery hall. He had been confident in his ability to centre himself, but his clumsiness with the bow suggested that his confidence was misplaced. It was dismaying and a little irritating to discover that Nichiren's training was not as thorough as it might have been.

Jimmu was given his own room on the ground floor of the castle. The other members of Lord Ankan's bodyguard were accommodated in the same corridor. Jimmu's room was small. His only possessions, his sword and sleeping mat, were brought from the barracks by a servant.

Jimmu pushed open the shutters and lounged against the sill. He could see the bridge over the pool where he had met Takeko in the moonlight. The sky was overcast, the air cold and still.

Where is my centre? thought Jimmu.

For many years, his centre had been Nichiren. He had followed Nichiren's orders, borne Nichiren's beatings, and treasured the rare occasions when he had earned Nichiren's approval. Everything had been done according to Nichiren's rule. Jimmu had never had to think for himself – until now.

Are you in Mitsukage Castle because you want to be, or because it's where Nichiren wanted you to be? thought Jimmu. Do you really want to avenge your father, or are you trying to please Nichiren? Is killing Lord Ankan really the best way to redeem your family's honour?

Jimmu had never questioned himself like this before, and he could not find the answers to his questions.

Snow began to fall. Silent flakes drifted lazily on the breeze.

A figure moved across the lawn, towards Jimmu. It was Takeko. She was wearing a long padded coat, leggings and a pair of mittens. Snowflakes caught in her hair.

Seeing her made Jimmu feel excited, and calm, and...

"I wish to speak with you," Takeko said.

Jimmu clambered over the sill, into the garden. His feet were bare, but he did not notice the cold. He was only aware of Takeko.

"I came because I knew you would appreciate the opportunity of thanking me," Takeko said.

"Thanking you for what, My Lady?" Jimmu enquired.

Takeko glared in disbelief.

"For your promotion," she said. "You don't believe that my father thought of it himself, do you? I told him to promote you, and I went on telling him until he did. I can be quite persuasive when I need to be."

Jimmu's wounded pride stung. He had thought Lord Ankan had been impressed by his courage and swordsmanship, instead Ankan had merely given in to his daughter's nagging.

"I'm very grateful to you, My Lady," he said, bowing low, but sounding sullen.

"It was nothing," Takeko said airily. "I merely paid off the debt I owe you. You saved my life at Zato, and I talked my father into making your dreams come true. Now you can train as a samurai. That makes us even."

"Yes, My Lady."

"So there's no reason for us to meet, or talk to each other again."

"No, My Lady," agreed Jimmu.

Takeko scowled.

"Is that the best you can come up with – *No, My Lady*?" she jeered. "Doesn't the idea of never meeting me again break your heart? Don't you want to perform a recklessly heroic act to gain my favour? That's what heroes do in stories."

"But I'm not a hero, My Lady," Jimmu pointed out, "and this is not a story."

"Well it ought to be!" snarled Takeko. "You should—"

She shut her mouth so smartly that her teeth clicked together.

"I should what, My Lady?" Jimmu said.

"I don't know!" said Takeko. "Stop pestering me! Why do you have to make everything so complicated?"

Without waiting for a reply, Takeko turned with a flounce, and hurried away into the dark, and the falling snow.

Jimmu was bewildered. There was no accounting for Takeko's changes of mood, and illogical rage.

Is she really angry with me, or just pretending? he wondered. And why do I want to know? Why should it matter to me?

But it did matter to him. Though he was not fully aware of it, something inside him had found its centre in Takeko.

Chapter 12
Mistukage Castle
ISE PROVINCE, WINTER 1572

For the next two months, Captain Muraki worked Jimmu hard. He was as demanding as Nichiren had been, but better at explaining the reasons behind his demands. Under his tutelage, Jimmu began to grasp why there was more to being a samurai than fighting.

Each morning, Jimmu rose before sunup, doused himself in cold water, and practised with his sword in the exercise yard until Captain Muraki joined him. Jimmu's archery improved, and he learned some of the finer points of fighting with a spear. If the captain's duties interrupted a session, Jimmu continued by himself.

But there were two concerns that no amount of training could keep out of his mind: avenging his father, and Takeko.

Nichiren had insisted that Jimmu should keep his

feelings strictly disciplined. Now that he was almost eighteen, Jimmu found this far trickier than when he had been a child. It seemed that his feelings did not care to be disciplined. He yearned for Takeko's attention and approval, and dreamed of her smile. Sometimes he indulged in wild fantasies in which he ran off with Takeko to live a simple life, like that of the peasants in the remote fishing village where he had grown up with Nichiren. Nichiren had scorned such lives as "meaningless", but the people who led them had seemed happy enough. Jimmu was disgusted with himself after these fantasies, and exercised even more vigorously, but there were moments when he regretted having to bear the heavy burden of his destiny.

Lord Ankan posed as knotty a problem. When he had first entered Mitsukage Castle, Jimmu had expected to act quickly. Since that had proved impossible, he had decided to wait for the perfect opportunity to present itself — or was he simply making excuses for his inaction? Surely, perfect opportunities had to be created?

One evening, as he was meditating in his room, Jimmu heard voices and laughter outside. Curious, he went to his window and peered through the shutters.

Takeko was in the garden near the archery hall, launching paper lanterns in the pool. Lord Ankan stood watching, and beside him was an elderly woman whom Jimmu took to be Lady Murasaki. Takeko giggled with delight as the lanterns glided across the surface of the water, her face as open as a child's. Lord Ankan was beaming. All his stiff formality had left him, and his eyes were full of affection for his daughter.

Jimmu felt as if he were intruding on a private moment, and looked away, aching with emptiness.

Why did my parents never care for me like that? he thought. Why did they leave me to face my fate alone? Was something wrong with me?

He tried to picture Lord Ankan as the fiend he had imagined when he was younger, but all he could see was Nichiren's face, rising up in his mind like smoke from a fire.

That evening, Jimmu received an unannounced visit from Captain Muraki, who spoke to him in a low urgent voice.

"Lady Takeko desires to visit the winter fair in Sakura," he said. "To disguise herself, she'll dress in plain clothes, like the daughter of a local squire. You will accompany her, as a guard."

"I am honoured, sir," said Jimmu, "but wouldn't a more experienced man be better suited to the task?"

Captain Muraki straightened his shoulders.

"Lord Ankan has issued a direct order, and you will obey him," he said.

"Yes, sir!"

"You will speak to no one of this, Jimmu. The fewer people who know, the smaller the risk to Lady Takeko," said the captain. He made to leave, but turned back at the doorway and said, "Be careful, Jimmu."

"Have you heard reports of Takeda soldiers near Sakura, sir?" asked Jimmu.

"No, but be careful nonetheless," Captain Muraki said, and turned away.

At daybreak, Jimmu and Takeko rode out of the castle, heading south-west, in the direction of the coast. It was a cold morning, and the sky was pale grey. The landscape's winter colours were sombre, streaked white with thin patches of snow.

Takeko's "disguise" turned out to be the same padded cotton outfit that she had worn when Jimmu had last seen her. Her hair was pinned up, and concealed beneath a wide-brimmed straw hat.

Jimmu was shy of Takeko, unable to think of anything to say, and when he looked at her, he felt hot and clumsy.

"You're quiet," observed Takeko. "Aren't you pleased that we're together again?"

"It's always a pleasure to serve you, My Lady," Jimmu said.

Takeko pouted.

"That isn't what I meant," she said. "And I told you before, I'm not 'My Lady' when we're outside the castle."

"As you wish."

Takeko peered intently at Jimmu.

"Say my name," she said.

"What?"

"I've never heard you say my name."

Jimmu blushed. "Takeko."

"I like the way you say it," said Takeko. "Names are powerful. If you tell a witch your name, she can use it to put a curse on you."

"I'll be sure to remember that if I ever meet any witches," Jimmu said drily.

"You might already have," teased Takeko. "I might be a witch for all you know."

Though Jimmu would not have been surprised to discover that Takeko was a witch, he made no reply.

"What do you dream about, Jimmu?" demanded Takeko.

"I don't know. Mostly things that I was frightened of when I was a child."

"What things?"

"Ghosts," Jimmu said. "Bloodsuckers. Demons in the night. What made you afraid when you were little?"

"Grandmother!" said Takeko. "She still frightens me sometimes. She pays the servants to spy on me and report back to her. She treats me like a baby. I knew she wouldn't approve of our being alone together like this. That's why I asked father to send you with me to Sakura."

"So I'm only here because you wanted to spite your grandmother?" said Jimmu.

"Of course!" Takeko retorted.

This answer both relieved and disappointed Jimmu.

"Not that I particularly object to being with you again," Takeko added. "Your company isn't repulsive to me – not entirely."

Jimmu was exasperated. Before he could stop himself, he said, "Are you really so conceited, or are you playing some sort of game?"

Takeko's face lit up.

"Ah, so you do answer back!" she said with a laugh. "And don't you dare apologize for doing it."

She seemed pleased.

The streets of Sakura were lined with stalls that offered a bewildering range of goods: fruit, sacks of rice and millet; rolls of rich silks; slices of candied yams, and steaming bowls of tea; incense and ink blocks.

Takeko wanted to see everything, and Jimmu had trouble keeping up with her as she darted from stall to stall. Eventually she bought a lacquered paper box as a gift for her father, and for herself, a small horse carved in red jade.

Jimmu was enchanted by the changing expressions on Takeko's face, and her infectious laughter. For a while, he was able to forget that he was her servant.

The hours passed quickly. After eating at a stall that sold hot soba noodles and seafood, it was time to leave.

As they walked along the crowded street, towards the spot where the horses were tethered, Jimmu lost his footing and collided with a richly dressed samurai, who flew into a rage.

"You idiot!" shouted the samurai. "Don't you have any control over yourself?"

Jimmu was irritated by the man's bullying tone, but kept his temper.

"I apologize for my clumsiness, sir," he said.

A knot of people had gathered, hoping to see a sword fight.

The samurai enjoyed the attention, and played up to his audience.

"I'm not sure that your apology is sufficient!" he blustered. "Contact with you has sullied my clothing.

I see you're wearing a sword. Is it for show, or do you know how to use it?"

The onlookers sidled backwards to get themselves out of harm's way.

The samurai's insulting question was a challenge and a few months earlier Jimmu would have risen to it, but he had Takeko to think of, so he exercised the restraint that Captain Muraki had recommended.

"Yes, sir, I know how to use my sword. I also know when to use it, and now is not the time," he said. "Kindly allow my mistress and me to leave in peace."

The samurai felt less sure of himself. He sensed the confidence that underlay Jimmu's calm politeness.

"Very well," he said. "You may count yourself lucky that I'm in a forgiving mood today."

The samurai continued down the street.

"You could have killed him," Takeko murmured.

"Perhaps," said Jimmu. "But I'm here to guard you, not fight duels."

Takeko smiled mischievously. "You always manage to surprise me, Jimmu, but one day I'll uncover your secret."

Jimmu felt an icy stab of alarm.

"My secret?" he gasped.

"Everybody has secrets," said Takeko.

Jimmu relaxed.

"And what's yours?" he enquired.

"Ah, wouldn't you like to know!" said Takeko.

On the return journey, it was Takeko's turn to be silent. Jimmu did not disturb her, but at last Takeko announced, "I don't want to go back to Mitsukage Castle, Jimmu."

"But it's your home," Jimmu pointed out. "Aren't you happy there?"

"I'm suffocating there!" Takeko growled. "You're the only thing about the place that isn't boring. You know what I wish?"

"What?"

"That I really was a local squire's daughter, and that you were a samurai," Takeko said. "Then we could be sweethearts."

Thinking that Takeko was joking, Jimmu laughed.

"Why would you want me for a sweetheart?" he said.

Takeko's eyes darkened with anger.

"Men are stupid!" she snapped. "They don't notice anything!"

She urged her horse into a gallop.

Jimmu galloped in pursuit. When he caught up with Takeko, he leaned across, grasped her horse's reins, and brought both their mounts to a halt.

Takeko glared sullenly. Her lips were tightly pursed.

Jimmu was shaking inside.

"Yes," he said, in a voice that he hardly recognized as his own.

"Yes what?"

"Yes, if you were a squire's daughter," mumbled Jimmu. "We could – what you said."

Takeko smiled.

The smile was as wide as the sky, and Jimmu lost himself in it.

Chapter 13
Mistukage Castle
ISE PROVINCE, WINTER 1572

Messengers from Lord Oda Nobunaga arrived daily at Mitsukage Castle, and they brought news of war. The Takeda forces had taken Futamata Castle, and were preparing to move south against Lord Tokugawa Ieyasu's fortress of Hamamatsu in Totomi province. Lord Ieyasu had asked Lord Nobunaga for reinforcements, and Lord Nobunaga had instructed Lord Ankan to march his men to Hamamatsu, and place them at Lord Ieyasu's disposal.

When Jimmu heard of this, he was convinced that it was a sign. Fate had determined that he must share a battlefield with Choju Ankan, and he intended that Ankan would die there, tasting neither the sweetness of victory in battle, nor the bitterness of defeat.

Mitsukage Castle prepared itself for conflict. Blacksmiths' hammers chimed day and night. Soldiers sharpened their weapons on whetstones. Provisions were made ready for loading onto packhorses. Captain Muraki abandoned tutoring Jimmu in order to oversee the drilling of new recruits. Jimmu continued his exercises, fencing with his shadow, which his imagination turned into Ankan the dragon.

During one solitary session in the exercise yard, Jimmu was interrupted by Takeko's maidservant.

"My Lady wishes to see you at the pool in the garden," said the maid. "You will go there now, and she will join you shortly."

Jimmu nodded in acknowledgement. He had struggled to control his feelings for Takeko, and it was time to bring the struggle to an end. What had passed between them on the road back from Sakura was an impossible dream. It was as if Takeko had cast a spell over him that day, and turned him into someone who was free to do as he wished with his life. Sweet as that dream had been, he must force himself to wake from it, and deny what he felt for Takeko.

We cannot be together, Jimmu thought. How could she ever love her father's killer? After I am dead, she will spit on my memory. The break must come.

Better now than on another day.

Though his mind was certain that this was the right decision, his emotions told him otherwise. The thought of not being with Takeko, never hearing her laugh, never looking in her eyes again, filled him with pain.

"Discipline yourself!" said a voice in his head. "Control your feelings. In a fight, self-control can be the difference between living and dying."

Oddly, Jimmu could not tell if the voice belonged to Nichiren, or Captain Muraki.

It was chilly in the garden. The bare branches of the cherry trees were stark against a sky the colour of pumice. Jimmu waited at the edge of the pool. He was glad of the cold, and wanted it to freeze him until his heart was solid and felt nothing. Down in the pool, his own reflection regarded him morosely.

Takeko's reflection slid over the surface of the water, and stood at his side. She was wearing a blue silk kimono under a thick red cape, and she looked more beautiful than Jimmu had ever seen her before.

"This is just like a scene in one of my favourite romances!" declared Takeko. "On the eve of battle, a handsome young samurai pays a secret visit to a princess, and confesses his undying love for her. Though she yearns to tell him that she loves him in return, the difference in their rank prevents her from speaking to him. The next day, the samurai is killed. The princess shuts herself away, and dies of grief. Isn't that beautiful?"

"It's only a story, My Lady," Jimmu said.

"My life should be a story!" sighed Takeko. "Are you going to pour out your heart to me?"

Jimmu steeled himself.

"You shouldn't say such things, My Lady," he said. "They are beneath you. We've both behaved like foolish children, but now we must grow up."

Takeko laughed.

"Ah!" she exclaimed. "You're playing the part of a faithful servant who realizes that his love for his mistress is doomed, and so—"

"I'm not playing, My Lady," Jimmu broke in.

Takeko was crestfallen.

"Don't you like me any more?" she whispered.

"My feelings are of no importance, but your reputation is," said Jimmu.

"Lady Takeko's reputation, you mean," Takeko said. "Lady Takeko has to be proper, and polite, and make herself attractive to a wealthy suitor. Lady Takeko is an item to be traded. But what about me, Jimmu – the real me? Yes, you and I started out as a game. I was bored, and it was fun to pretend with you, but what happens when the pretence becomes reality?"

Jimmu deliberately made his voice harsh.

"Pretence can never be true, My Lady," he said. "The truth is that I am a servant, and you are a noblewoman of the Choju family."

Takeko seethed with fury.

"Then tell me you don't care about me, and I'll leave you alone!" she snapped.

Jimmu looked straight at Takeko, hoping that the expression in his eyes would reveal nothing of his true emotions.

"I don't care about you, My Lady," he lied.

"I don't believe you!" said Takeko.

Her red cape swirled as she turned and walked away.

On the morning of the departure for Hamamatsu, Jimmu, uncomfortable in his newly fitted armour, lined up in the main courtyard with the other troops, while priests chanted blessings. When the chanting ended, Lord Ankan appeared in full battle gear, his war fan opened to reveal the crest of the Choju family.

With one voice, the soldiers called on him to lead them to glory. "Ei!"

And he answered them yes. "O!"

"Ei!"

"O!"

"Ei!"

"O!"

Jimmu found it impossible not to be caught up in the atmosphere. The soldiers around him were no longer strangers, but comrades who would march together and face death together. Jimmu was proud to be among them and, for the first time in his life, felt that he was part of something.

Lord Ankan completed the final ritual. As he passed through the outer gates, he stepped over a kitchen knife, a gesture believed to protect his home from attack in his absence. Then he mounted his horse, and the troops set off.

Jimmu rode out of the castle. He wondered if Takeko might be watching from the battlements, but he did not turn to look back.

What would be the point? he thought. I'll never see her again.

That evening, Lord Ankan's troops made camp in a river meadow. The men lit fires, and the foot soldiers used their iron helmets as cooking pots for their rice ration.

After eating, Captain Muraki relaxed near the fire outside his tent, but Jimmu could not settle. He sat down, wriggled, stood up, and paced to and fro, feeding branches to the fire.

"What's troubling you?" asked the captain.

Jimmu hunkered down and peered at the red shapes that shimmered at the core of the flames.

"I've never fought in a battle before," he said. "I'm not afraid, but I'm worried that I may do the wrong thing."

Captain Muraki smiled.

"Stay close to me, and you won't," he said. "Accept that you may be wounded or killed, and you will be free to concentrate on the moment. In battle, there is only the moment. Besides, I can see your future."

"You can?"

"Certainly," said the captain. "You will fight outstandingly well. Lord Ankan will mention your name in dispatches to Lord Nobunaga, and Lord Nobunaga will petition the Emperor to make you a samurai — though the petition will be more like an order."

Jimmu did not reply.

Captain Muraki is wrong, he thought. I don't have a future. When Choju Ankan's life ends, so will mine.

Chapter 14
Hamamatsu Castle
TOTOMI PROVINCE, WINTER 1572

*L*ate in the afternoon of the next day, Lord Ankan and his men arrived at Hamamatsu. The fortress was not as impressive as Mitsukage Castle, though it was larger, and its central keep was more imposing. Outside the walls stood a small town of tents.

Jimmu had never seen so many soldiers in one place, and was staggered. Wherever he turned he saw strutting samurai – some with personal attendants – companies of spearmen drilling, musketeers carrying their weapons on their shoulders, archers and infantrymen. Messengers with silk pennants attached to the back plates of their armour galloped in all directions.

Jimmu began to appreciate the power of a great lord.

"How can Tokugawa Ieyasu control so many?" he gasped.

"He can't," said Captain Muraki. "Lord Ieyasu

controls the generals, who control the captains, and so on right down to the men who drive the packhorses. That's why soldiers are drilled so often. It teaches them to act together. Without discipline, an army turns into a mob."

"But with so many different commanders, don't you get mixed up about who you're fighting?" said Jimmu.

Captain Muraki laughed.

"The enemy is easily identified," he said. "His soldiers are the ones who are trying to kill you."

Lord Ankan selected a site for his men to set up camp, then rode inside Hamamatsu to confer with Lord Ieyasu and his generals.

At dusk, the lights of the camp stretched into the distance like a galaxy of orange stars. The air was pungent with the scent of woodsmoke. Jimmu and Captain Muraki took their evening meal together, and were joined by Sergeant Hankei.

"I've never known such a place for rumours!" asserted the sergeant. "We've only been here an hour or so, but I've already heard that the Takeda have given up and gone home, that Lord Ieyasu has been slain by an assassin, and that Lord Nobunaga is on his way with an army of fifty thousand."

"Which story do you believe?" Jimmu asked.

"None of them!" snorted Sergeant Hankei. "Before a battle, you hear all sorts of wild tales. Most of the rumours are spread by enemy spies, hoping to undermine morale."

"And our spies are in the Takeda camp, doing the same thing," Captain Muraki added.

Jimmu grimaced. "Can nobody's word be trusted?"

Captain Muraki gestured emphatically. "Trust Lord Ankan," he said. "He speaks plainly and honestly to his men." He stood up. "I must visit the latrine. If a messenger comes for me, instruct him to wait."

As the captain strode off between the tents, Jimmu turned to Sergeant Hankei.

"Is he right?" he said. "Can we trust what Lord Ankan tells us?"

Sergeant Hankei shrugged. "Ishida Muraki is devoted to His Lordship. When the captain was wounded at the battle of Moribe, Lord Ankan had him carried back to Mitsukage in his own palanquin. He hired the finest physicians in Kyoto to save the captain's leg."

Once again Jimmu felt at odds with himself. Captain Muraki and Sergeant Hankei were obviously sincere in their respect for Lord Ankan, a respect that did not square with the contempt for the man which Nichiren had instilled in Jimmu.

He can't be cruel and considerate at the same time! Jimmu reasoned. Perhaps he was once a monster, but something happened to change him, and if he is no longer the same person who plotted my father's death, how justified am I in taking revenge on him?

There was another far worse possibility...that Nichiren had lied to him. If Nichiren had lied, then Jimmu's whole life was a lie, and Jimmu refused to accept it. No! he told himself. Captain Muraki and Sergeant Hankei have been taken in by Lord Ankan's charm. I must be stronger than that.

North of Hamamatsu the ground sloped upwards, then levelled out into a broad plain that was cut in two by a narrow gorge. The Takeda army had crossed the gorge the previous day, and pitched their camp in front of it. Though the camp was not visible from the castle, parties of scouts reported back on its activity during the night.

The following morning, just after dawn, the army of Tokugawa Ieyasu stood up before his battle standard. The standard was in the shape of a huge golden fan, made from stiffened paper. Both sides of the fan were decorated with a red disc, to represent the rising sun.

The proceedings were witnessed by Lord Ieyasu, who sat with his generals in a semicircle. Servants brought them a ceremonial meal of dried chestnuts, followed by seaweed, shellfish and cups of sake. When the meal was over, Lord Ieyasu got to his feet and stood in plain view of his men. He was young, barely out of his twenties, but he had the dignified bearing of a great lord. The shape of his breastplate and helmet had been copied from European armour.

Lord Ieyasu slowly lifted his battle fan. Flags were raised, conch shells bellowed and drums throbbed.

The troops marched off to war.

Jimmu was moved by the spectacle.

"Today, we're going to win a great victory over

the Takeda!" he exclaimed to Captain Muraki.

"I envy you your certainty, Jimmu," replied the captain. "I'm not so sure myself. I've heard that the Takeda outnumber us more than three to one. We'll have a hard fight of it."

"Another campfire rumour!" Jimmu scoffed.

"No," said the captain. "The information was given to me by Lord Ankan."

A momentary panic gripped Jimmu – if he were killed by a Takeda soldier, his father would never be avenged.

"Pull yourself together!" said a voice in his head. "You are behaving like a coward. You will survive the battle by making proper use of your fighting skills. Afterwards, you will bring the beast Ankan to justice. He caused the death of your noble father. Your mother swallowed poison because of him, and died a slow, agonizing death. You have a sacred purpose. No bullet or arrow will come near you. Any enemy who challenges you will fall. You will kill Ankan with your father's sword."

There was no mistaking the voice in Jimmu's mind; it was Nichiren's.

✧

When the opposing sides came within sight of each other, they hurriedly assumed their battle formations. In the teeth of a bitter wind the masses of armed men swirled like flocks of starlings on the wing. The Tokugawa army advanced to within seventy metres of the Takeda camp.

Lord Ankan's soldiers were positioned on the left flank of the Tokugawa forces, together with the troops of General Ietada, General Tadakatsu and General Kazumasa, who were also allies of Lord Ieyasu. Jimmu was given command of a detail of fifteen spearmen, one of whom was Kambei.

Kambei grinned at Jimmu, but the expression in his eyes revealed the grin as no more than bravado.

"The shoe's on the other foot now, eh, lad?" he chuckled. "Today you give the orders, and I jump — not for long though. We're going to be slaughtered."

"Empty your mind of such thoughts!" commanded Jimmu. "You'll need a clear head for what's to come."

"I've never had a clear head in my life, but I know death when I see it," Kambei responded. "Our guts are going to get trampled under the hoofs of the Takeda cavalry."

"That's enough, guardsman!" snapped Jimmu. "Your loose talk is making your comrades nervous."

Kambei lowered his head and spat with casual contempt, but he kept quiet.

The busy manoeuvring was succeeded by a long period of inactivity, during which tension built up until it was almost unbearable.

Captain Muraki stopped by to conduct a routine inspection.

"Is everything in order?" he enquired.

"Yes, sir. The men have been ready for over an hour," said Jimmu. "Why don't the Takeda attack? They have superior numbers, what are they waiting for?"

"Takeda Shingen remains true to his motto, and stands as still as a mountain," said Captain Muraki. "Lord Ieyasu has taken up a strong defensive position. The Takeda will bide their time, unless something happens to change the situation."

Snowflakes started to fall, flurrying in the wind.

Captain Muraki looked up at the sky.

"That's it!" he said. "If this snow settles, it will hamper the Takeda cavalry. Prepare yourself, Jimmu!"

The captain had hardly finished speaking before muskets began to crackle.

Chapter 15

Outside Hamamatsu Castle

TOTOMI PROVINCE, WINTER 1572

Snowflakes blew into Jimmu's eyes and melted into rainbow colours when he blinked. He heard one of his men murmuring a prayer, the chattering teeth of another man, and the rumble of approaching hoofbeats.

Jimmu drew on what he had learned from Captain Muraki, and concentrated until a strange calm crept over him. Everything that followed seemed unreal, as if a dream were being acted out in front of him.

Takeda cavalrymen loomed up out of the swirling snow. Some drew on bows, some wielded long swords. They had the faces of grimacing demons.

A horse fell screaming, its legs buckling, mane and tail flowing as it crashed to the ground. The thrown rider appeared to float on air for an instant, before another rider's horse trampled over him.

"Lower spears!" commanded Jimmu, his voice sounding as terse and gruff as Nichiren's.

The spearmen obeyed, and then a cavalryman burst upon them, his sword slashing, trying to keep off the merciless points of the spears that jabbed at him. A spearman collapsed in a spray of blood. The cavalryman tumbled from his saddle.

Jimmu sprang forward and thrust his sword through a gap in the fallen man's armour. The blade grated on bone. Life drained out of the cavalryman's eyes.

The spearmen readied themselves for another horseman.

Jimmu entered a trancelike state. He felt detached from the falling snow, the choking-sweet smell of gunpowder smoke, the latrine-stink of death. The air was filled with the sound of clashing weapons, and the agonized cries of the wounded. Riderless horses with foaming mouths galloped by. None of it made any sense to Jimmu. He was numb.

Twice more he was called on to dispatch an unseated cavalryman, and then the Takeda switched their attention to another section of the line. Jimmu's men took time to catch their breath, and bind their wounds.

Kambei hunkered down to address the corpse of a comrade.

"Goodbye, Beni!" he rasped. "We had good laughs together. If I live to drink sake again, I'll get drunk in your honour. I'm sorry you're dead, but rather you than me, my friend."

Captain Muraki appeared at Jimmu's side.

"Casualties?" he enquired briskly.

"Two dead, sir," Jimmu replied. "Three Takeda killed."

The captain leaned closer and spoke confidentially.

"You fought well," he said. "Lord Ankan has expressed his satisfaction with your conduct."

Jimmu, now reconciled to his hidden purpose, bowed his head so that Captain Muraki would not catch his dark smile. Choju Ankan was not the only one capable of practising deception.

"His Lordship's generous praise humbles me," Jimmu said.

A sudden clamour of drums and wailing conches caused him to look up.

"What does it mean?" he asked.

Captain Muraki's face was impassive.

"It's the signal to retreat," he said. "Order your men to fall back, then fetch your horse and fall back yourself."

"Fall back to where?" asked Jimmu.

"Hamamatsu, if need be," replied the captain. "The Takeda army has the upper hand."

The snow stopped, but the wind still blew keenly. Jimmu rode south across a nightmare landscape that gleamed white and ghostly in the gathering dusk. Retreating soldiers resembled lines of foraging ants.

Jimmu tried to imagine what Lord Ankan was feeling.

Is he shamed by the defeat, or is he angry? he thought. Maybe he's already scheming to turn the situation to his advantage. Will he betray Tokugawa Ieyasu, as he betrayed my father?

The question helped him to concentrate on the hatred that Nichiren had nurtured in him.

Jimmu found Captain Muraki and Lord Ankan in

company with Lord Ieyasu and several generals. The Tokugawa standard had been raised on the crest of the slope that ran down to Hamamatsu, and troops were rallying to it, though there were few of them as yet.

Lord Ieyasu was ill at ease, and his horse mirrored his mood. The animal kept jerking its head, and stamping its hoofs.

"Where is General Tadakatsu?" Lord Ieyasu demanded.

"When I last saw him, he and his men were completely surrounded by Takeda cavalry," said one of the generals.

Lord Ieyasu stretched his mouth into a grim line, reined in his mount, and stretched out his battle fan.

"We must gather our troops without delay!" he cried. "I will lead a charge into the enemy ranks, cut my way through to General Tadakatsu and perish fighting by his side."

The generals glanced at one another in alarm, but Lord Ankan was the only one who dared to speak up. He unfastened his mask so that his voice could be heard clearly, and said, "No one questions your valour, but this is a moment to apply wisdom, My

Lord. You have suffered a defeat, but you can avoid a massacre. There are not enough men here to mount a successful charge. If you are killed, Hamamatsu will fall, and the Takeda will gain control of the entire Totomi province. I respectfully submit that it is your duty to return to the fortress."

The generals grunted and nodded to indicate their agreement.

"I will remain with these troops, and fight a rearguard action," continued Lord Ankan. "That should give you the time to reach Hamamatsu and begin organizing its defence."

Jimmu was dumbfounded. Lord Ankan had spoken like a brave man who was willing to die for his ally.

Then Captain Muraki urged his horse forward.

"No, My Lord," he said to Lord Ankan. "I will stay and fight. You must go with Lord Ieyasu."

Lord Ankan was furious.

"Do you presume to give me orders, captain!" he spluttered. "It seems that you have forgotten your place!"

"Far from it, My Lord," Captain Muraki replied evenly. "You said yourself that this is a moment for wisdom. Lord Ieyasu may have need of your advice. He won't get it if you're lying dead here."

"He's right, Ankan," commented one of the generals. "Better a living general than a valiant cadaver."

Jimmu stared hard at Lord Ankan. Had he known that Captain Muraki would volunteer to take his place? Had his offer to lead the rearguard action been a sham?

Lord Ankan's face gave nothing away.

"I salute you, Ishida Muraki!" he said hoarsely. "I commend your spirit to your ancestors."

Lord Ankan turned his horse, and rode down the slope, behind Lord Ieyasu and the generals. The nobles' personal bodyguards followed on.

Jimmu rode up to Captain Muraki.

"How can I assist you, sir?" he said.

Realization struck him like a blow. What was he thinking of? The words seemed to have sprung from his lips of their own accord. His admiration for Captain Muraki had overcome his desire for revenge. What had happened to his values? Where was his iron resolve? Did he really respect Ishida Muraki more than the memory of his father?

Captain Muraki frowned.

"You can do nothing, Jimmu," he said. "Go with Lord Ankan, and protect him."

"But—"

"Every samurai knows that one day he will come to the place where he must die," said Captain Muraki. "This is my place – not yours, Jimmu."

Jimmu was moved to tears, but he held them back. "How can I thank you for all you've taught me?"

"By fighting fearlessly and devoting yourself to Lord Ankan," Captain Muraki said. "Now go!"

As Jimmu's horse descended the slope, his resentment and anger grew. Lord Ankan had brought about the deaths of his mother and father, and now Captain Muraki was about to sacrifice himself.

Ankan is not worthy! Jimmu thought. Captain Muraki is worth a thousand men of his sort.

Jimmu ground his teeth. He was determined that before the break of dawn, he would slay Choju Ankan.

Chapter 16
Hamamatsu Castle
TOTOMI PROVINCE, WINTER 1572

Jimmu lost the trail in the dark, and blundered into a dense thicket of bamboo. By the time he forced his way out he was thoroughly disorientated, and might have spent the entire night wandering about, had he not spotted the lights of Hamamatsu burning brightly on the plain below the ridge. In fact the lights were so bright that Jimmu feared that the Takeda had already taken the fortress, and left it in flames. He encouraged his horse onwards, down the steep slope.

However, as he drew nearer to the stronghold, Jimmu was reassured to see that he had been mistaken. Hamamatsu was not on fire, but ablaze with light. The walls were lined with flaming torches and braziers, and bonfires had been lit on either side of the approach to the main gates, which stood wide open. The fortress had been transformed into a beacon to guide the scattered Tokugawa troops to safety, and as if this were not enough, from within the walls came the beating of great drums.

Jimmu rode in through the gateway, expecting Hamamatsu's main courtyard to be a solid mass of soldiers, but to his astonishment it was almost deserted. A few armed men scurried about, apparently at random. Archers and musketeers were spaced widely apart along the battlements. A handful of officers bawled out orders.

Mystified, Jimmu found a hitching post, dismounted, and tethered his horse.

Almost at once he was accosted by a captain whose armour bore the Tokugawa badge. The captain thrust a bow and a quiver of arrows on Jimmu.

"Here, take these and join the defences on the north wall!" barked the captain.

"But where is our army?" asked Jimmu.

The captain smiled ironically.

"This *is* our army," he replied. "The rest are still on their way back. There are two hundred of us at most, and the Takeda have ten thousand cavalrymen alone. Go quickly now! There isn't much time."

Jimmu made his way up to the battlements on the north wall, where he was amazed to be reunited with Kambei.

"Kambei?" he gasped. "How did you get here?"

"As quickly as I could," retorted Kambei. "Our detail came under cavalry attack. I got separated from the others, and headed back to Hamamatsu."

"Did you see Captain Muraki?" Jimmu said.

Kambei shrugged.

"I was too busy running to see anything," he confessed.

Jimmu frowned at the torches, the braziers, and the thin spread of men.

"What's going on, Kambei?" he said. "Why haven't the gates been closed? Why have so many torches been lit? This is more like a festival than the preparation for a siege."

Kambei chuckled wheezily.

"This is all Lord Ankan's idea!" he announced. "It's a bluff. The lights and drums will draw our men back, but they'll draw the Takeda too. When they see the open gates, they'll suspect a trap. What lord would be stupid enough to leave his main gates wide open to the enemy, unless thousands of men were hiding inside?" Kambei chuckled again. "Choju Ankan is a wily one!"

Nichiren's voice grated inside Jimmu's head. "It is a coward's plan! A brave lord would fight to the death rather than bear the shame of defeat."

Jimmu shut out the voice. He strung his bow, notched an arrow in place, and stared out at the night. Retreating Tokugawa soldiers straggled continuously through the gates, but the garrison was nowhere near strong enough to withstand the might of the Takeda. If Lord Ankan's plan failed, the Tokugawa and their allies would be wiped out.

A few minutes passed in what seemed like a year, then the flow of stragglers abruptly stopped, and the sound of advancing horsemen swelled in the darkness.

"Here they come!" muttered Kambei.

The most distant bonfires winked as passing cavalrymen interrupted their light. The advance slowed when the riders registered the open gates of the fort, and came to a halt outside musket range. Firelight gleamed on metal; silken banners fluttered in the freezing wind.

Jimmu could almost hear the astonishment of the Takeda generals.

"Lord Shingen's out there somewhere," said Kambei. "He's calculating the odds. What's the strength of his enemy? How many casualties will he suffer if he storms Hamamatsu? If he loses too many men, how long will it be before Oda Nobunaga attacks him?"

Down in the courtyard someone raised a cheer. It spread through the fortress, until at last everyone was cheering. The cheer sounded scornful, defiant, the voice of an army that was confident of victory, and it evidently proved too much for Takeda Shingen. The cavalry turned about, and headed back for their camp near the gorge.

The volume of the cheering in Hamamatsu increased as men vented their relief.

Kambei hopped gleefully from foot to foot.

"Didn't I tell you?" he crowed. "Lord Ankan could show a fox a trick or two. Plenty of women will bless him for saving the lives of their husbands and sons, eh, Jimmu?"

Jimmu was too tired to answer, too tired to think; his mind was blank.

Jimmu fell asleep with his back resting against the battlements. Scraps of the day's events came back to him in disjointed dreams: the expression in the eyes of the Takeda cavalrymen he had finished off; a spearman screaming as he tumbled; Captain Muraki's air of resignation. Jimmu's limbs twitched, and he mumbled to himself.

Kambei woke Jimmu, and presented him with a bowl of hot barley soup.

"Get that inside you," Kambei advised. "It'll help keep out the cold."

Jimmu carefully blew on the surface of the soup before he sipped it.

"How long was I asleep?" he said.

"A couple of hours, maybe three," said Kambei.

Jimmu became awake enough to notice that Kambei was on edge and could not keep still.

"What's wrong?" demanded Jimmu.

"Lord Ankan has sent round a messenger to ask for a hundred volunteers," Kambei said.

"Volunteers for what?"

"Why don't we go and find out?" Kambei suggested.

Jimmu swallowed another mouthful of soup. Its warmth filled him with a sense of well-being.

"Of course," he said, standing.

Kambei and Jimmu went down to the courtyard, where they joined the rear of a large group of samurai and infantrymen. Lord Ankan was standing in the back of a cart, holding a blazing torch to illuminate his face.

"Thank you for accepting my invitation," he said. "Allow me to outline the present situation as I see it. Takeda Shingen and his army are far from home, and their supply lines are badly stretched. If he had taken Hamamatsu, he would have built up its defences, and eked out his stores until the spring. But he did not take Hamamatsu, and his reluctance to attack it shows that he is in a cautious frame of mind. He knows that the worst of the winter weather is on the way, and he does not want his army camping in the open when it arrives. I believe that if a small force raided the Takeda camp tonight, it would convince Lord Shingen that our numbers are greater than is actually the case, and he would return home. You are that small force, and I will lead you."

"Has Lord Ieyasu approved your plan, My Lord?" a voice called out.

Lord Ankan grinned like a naughty child.

"I have neglected to inform Lord Ieyasu of my intentions," he said. "His Lordship maintains that generals should keep well back from the front line. I do not agree with him. None of you is bound to accompany me. Any who wish to leave may do so now without shame, and without harming their reputation."

No one moved.

Lord Ankan saluted the men's courage by bowing to them.

"Very well," he said. "We will proceed on foot, as quietly as we can. Arm yourselves, and return here."

Most of the men dispersed to fetch their weapons. Those who were already armed stayed behind, including Kambei and Jimmu, who were spotted by Lord Ankan.

"Is that you, Kambei?" he said.

"It is, My Lord."

Lord Ankan craned his neck. "And who is that with you?"

"Jimmu," said Kambei.

"Ah, yes!" Lord Ankan said. "My budding samurai. Are you eager to prove yourself, young man?"

"Nothing could keep me from your side tonight, My Lord," Jimmu replied.

He pushed aside the doubts that clamoured in his mind. His instincts told him that the final confrontation with Choju Ankan was close at hand.

Chapter 17

Outside Hamamatsu Castle
TOTOMI PROVINCE, WINTER 1572

The raiding party slipped out of the side gate of Hamamatsu in ones and twos, keeping low in case of watching Takeda scouts. The men reassembled well away from the light of the bonfires, and lined up in double file before setting out at a jogtrot. True to his word, Lord Ankan took the lead.

Kambei and Jimmu went side by side. The party travelled in silence, and Jimmu was able to reflect without any distractions.

He heard Nichiren speaking his thoughts in an uncannily clear voice, so that it was as if Jimmu were listening to a ghost.

"During the attack it will be dark, and there will be uproar. It should be simple for you to find Ankan, call him out and put him to the sword. Afterwards, you must commit seppuku. Your father will be the first to greet you in the next life."

My father? Jimmu thought. Who was he? I hardly knew him, only what Nichiren told me about him. My parents never gave me advice, or comforted me when I was sad, or nursed me when I was sick. I've led my life for the benefit of two dead strangers. Why should I want to avenge them?

"What other purpose do you have?" said the voice of Nichiren. "What is the point of your life, if not to die? Without revenge, you are an insect crushed by a peasant's heel, a thing without honour, meaning or value. Only Ankan's blood can make you worthy."

Nichiren had said this, or something like it, almost every day when Jimmu was growing up, and Jimmu had believed him. Yet Ishida Muraki had seen worth in Jimmu. The captain had patiently trained him, and had been closer to a friend than anyone Jimmu had known. And Takeko: Jimmu remembered how her face had looked the last time he saw it – troubled, angry, sad. If someone as beautiful as Takeko cared about him, surely he could not be worthless?

The raiding party reached the scene of the afternoon's fighting. The moon emerged from behind a cloud and shone down on the carnage, its light turning the bloodstains on the snow black, and making statues of the dead.

Jimmu shivered. It seemed that they were trespassers in the land of the dead, and that at any second a corpse would leap to its feet and scream at them.

Lord Ankan suddenly stopped and looked down. The soldiers gathered around, and Jimmu saw that Lord Ankan was staring at the body of Captain Muraki.

The captain was lying on his back. His face was unmarked, but a spear with a broken shaft protruded from his breastplate. The dead Takeda troops littered close by showed how courageously he and his men had fought.

Earlier, when he had taken his leave of Captain Muraki, Jimmu had been able to control his emotions, but he could not control them any longer. He wept silently, his tears drying rapidly in the biting wind.

Lord Ankan raised his hand in a gesture of farewell to the captain, and as he turned away, Jimmu was astounded to see that he too had tears in his eyes.

Like me, he is grieving for Ishida Muraki, Jimmu thought.

It was disturbing to realize that he and Choju Ankan had something in common.

Once they were past the battlefield, the raiding party swung to the east of the Takeda camp. The sweep of the enemy's watchfires was awe-inspiring.

Lord Ankan gathered the men around him, out of earshot of the Takeda guards. He spoke quietly, but distinctly.

"No battle cries, no duelling and no prisoners," he said. "Our aim is not to gain glory, but to provoke the maximum disruption. Scatter fires, loose horses, and disappear into the night. Try to stay in groups. If you find yourself alone, return immediately to Hamamatsu. Above all, don't allow yourself to be captured." Lord Ankan drew his sword. "Attack!" he hissed.

The Takeda were taken unawares. Jimmu cut down a perimeter guard before the man could lower his spear. He plucked a brand from the watchfire and used it to set ablaze the silk tent of a samurai.

More tents burst into flames, like fiery flowers opening their petals. Men ran half asleep, or died attempting to rise from slumber. Horses galloped wildly, their eyes rolling in fear. The Tokugawa raiders stole like shadows through the camp, trailing death behind them. Panic spread among the Takeda. Cries of pain mingled with shouts of bewilderment.

Jimmu and Kambei fought as a team, watching each other's backs, giving each other warnings.

"On your right!" Kambei shouted.

Jimmu turned. A half-naked Takeda samurai was running at him, holding a spear with a long blade, like a sword. At the last moment Jimmu dodged, but the samurai anticipated the movement. The edge of the blade sliced through Jimmu's armour and gashed his left side above the hip. Jimmu grasped the shaft of the spear, calmly stepped forwards, and slashed the samurai's throat with a flick of his sword.

"Jimmu, you're hurt!" cried Kambei.

There was no pain yet, but there was blood. Jimmu felt a warm wetness spread over his left hip, and down onto his upper thigh. He did not have to look at the wound to know that it was serious, perhaps fatal.

A sense of urgency filled him. Time was running out. Would he die without avenging the death of his father?

"It's nothing," he said to Kambei. "I must go to Lord Ankan."

"Let me dress that wound first," offered Kambei.

"Later!" Jimmu insisted. "Where is Lord Ankan? I have a message for him."

"He's over there," said Kambei, pointing.

Lord Ankan was standing near a watchfire, looking around in an agitated manner. As Jimmu approached, Lord Ankan greeted him.

"Ah, Jimmu!" he said. "Help me to gather the men together. The Takeda must be preparing a counter-attack by now. We must return to Hamamatsu."

Jimmu felt his wound throbbing in time with the beating of his heart. He raised his sword so that the blade was parallel with his left cheek. The pain in his side sharpened, and seared.

"Defend yourself, Choju Ankan!" he snarled.

Lord Ankan instinctively drew his sword, and when Jimmu struck at him, he parried the blow with great skill.

"Are you mad, Jimmu?" he gasped. "What is the meaning of this?"

In reply, Jimmu swung his sword again. Lord Ankan locked blades with him, and their faces came close together.

"You are bleeding badly, Jimmu!" gasped Lord Ankan. "The pain of your wound has turned your wits. Lay down your sword, I have no wish to kill you."

Jimmu felt light-headed.

"Why not?" he cried. "You killed my father. I am Shimomura Jimmu, son of Lord Shimomura Kensu," he declared, "the man whose reputation you destroyed with forged documents, the man you drove to suicide, along with his wife, my mother!"

"What madness is this?" shouted Lord Ankan. "What are you talking about?"

Jimmu no longer knew himself; all his clear-cut certainties were blurred and blunted. As his strength ebbed away, so did his determination. Nichiren had taught him to hate Lord Ankan, but where was the demon Nichiren had described? Lord Ankan had treated Jimmu generously, and had displayed courage and skill in battle. With a sense of shock, Jimmu realized that Choju Ankan had earned his respect.

The shock was too great for Jimmu to bear. He flung his sword aside in a gesture of surrender, then felt his knees begin to buckle. The pain of his wound roared in a rising tide of darkness that swallowed him down.

Jimmu's mind entered a dream that seemed as real as waking. He was following a narrow mountain track that ran through a forest of firs. The track was scattered with browned pine needles and fallen cones. It passed by mossy boulders and clumps of brambles with sickly yellow leaves. Through gaps between the trees, Jimmu glimpsed a deep valley filled with white mist.

He stopped to look closely at a stump that stood beside the track. The stump had been carved into the likeness of a human figure, but the carving was so crude that it was impossible to tell whether the figure was intended to be male or female. At the foot of the stump, a bunch of flowers lay on a flat stone. The place was obviously a shrine, but Jimmu did not know which spirit was honoured there.

He bowed to the carving.

"Since I don't have an offering, I can't ask you for a blessing," he confessed to it, "so instead, I ask you please to leave me alone."

The sound of nearby laughter made him turn to his right. A short distance from the track, on the mountain's downward slope, the Takeda samurai who had wounded Jimmu was displaying his throat to Sadamichi. There was a dark rope-mark on Sadamichi's neck and his head hung awry, his left cheek resting on his left shoulder. When he noticed Jimmu, Sadamichi raised his right arm to show the bloodstained rags wrapped around the stump of his wrist.

"Eh, Farm Boy!" he jeered. "Have you come to cut off the other one?"

The samurai's throat bubbled as he laughed.

"Which direction should I take?" asked Jimmu.

"It doesn't matter," Sadamichi replied. "Wherever you go, you'll end up in the same place as the rest of us."

"What place?"

"The place where you die," Sadamichi said.

Jimmu walked on. The track rose steeply for a while, then levelled out. He passed through blades of dusty sunlight, but when the light touched his skin he felt no warmth. Before long, he came upon a group of men seated around a burned-out fire. Some of the men were the samurai Jimmu had fought at Zato, the rest were the bandits he had slain in the forest near the road to Kyoto.

Toshiro, the bandits' leader, scowled.

"What are you doing here?" he demanded.

"I'm lost," said Jimmu. "I'm not sure where I'm going."

Toshiro bared his bloodstained teeth in a smile.

"You'll never know until you make up your mind," he said. "It's your decision. It always has been. You shouldn't be with us. You belong where things happen. Nothing changes here, and the nothing goes on for ever. Get out while you still can."

"But I don't know the way out!" protested Jimmu.

"Yes you do," Toshiro said. "The way out is to live for as long as possible. Stay here much longer, and you'll be as dead as we are."

Jimmu sighed.

"It must be peaceful to be dead, and have no worries," he said.

"It isn't," Toshiro informed him. "The living find peace, not the dead. The dead aren't at peace. They aren't anything or anywhere. Don't be stupid. Go back to your life and live it."

Jimmu left the men and continued along the track, which gradually faded into darkness.

First came the rattle and drip of falling rain, then booming voices and footsteps. The air was peppery with a scent that matched the bitter taste in the mouth. A tongue moved over teeth.

My tongue, thought Jimmu. My teeth. My mouth.

He opened his eyes and saw his room in Mitsukage Castle. A cotton quilt had been drawn over him. His sword stood in the corner. Kambei was seated at his side.

"Are we dead?" whispered Jimmu.

"I don't think so," Kambei said.

Jimmu's shame pressed down on him.

"It would be better if I had died!" he said.

"If you knew the truth about me——"

"The truth is that the courage you showed the night of the raid on the Takeda camp helped turn back Takeda Shingen and his army, and save Hamamatsu," interrupted Kambei. "During the fighting, you were wounded, and you've been unconscious for six days. His Lordship's personal physician has been attending you. I've been ordered to watch over you, which I don't mind, because it's easier than guard duty."

"Did Lord Ankan say anything about me?" said Jimmu.

Kambei shrugged. "I think he is concerned for your health."

Jimmu was baffled. Why had Lord Ankan bothered to keep him alive? Was there going to be some sort of trial?

"But didn't Lord Ankan——" he said.

Kambei raised his hand.

"Rest!" he said gently. "There'll be plenty of time for talking after you get your strength back."

While Jimmu recovered, the winter turned severe. Blizzards raged for days on end, and the wind piled deep snowdrifts against the castle's outer walls. Long icicles hung from the eaves, and the pool in the garden froze over.

The wound in Jimmu's side healed quickly, but the wounds in his mind festered. He was doomed. His attempt on Lord Ankan's life had failed, and since he was too weak to escape from Mitsukage Castle, he could do nothing but accept whatever fate Lord Ankan had prepared for him. His prospects appeared as bleak and empty as the winter countryside. It would not be the glorious death he had foreseen for himself. All his training, planning and struggle had been for nothing. His life would end in shame and disgrace.

Kambei visited Jimmu daily, bringing food and keeping him company.

One evening, just after Jimmu and Kambei had finished supper, there was a knock on the screen door of Jimmu's room. Kambei slid back the door to reveal Lord Ankan standing in the corridor.

Kambei bowed low. "Good evening, My Lord."

"Good evening," said Lord Ankan. "Please leave

us, Kambei. I need to speak to Jimmu in private."

Kambei hurried away, and Lord Ankan stepped into the room.

Jimmu struggled onto all fours, and pressed his forehead against the floor.

Lord Ankan sat cross-legged in front of him.

"Get up, Jimmu," he said quietly.

"I can't!" burst out Jimmu. "How can I look you in the face after what I've done? Why haven't you had me put to death?"

"Get up," Lord Ankan said again.

Jimmu obediently raised his head.

Lord Ankan was dressed in a plain brown robe. His expression showed no sign of anger or hatred, and his voice was calm as he said, "There is a misunderstanding between us, which I am anxious to clear away. At Hamamatsu you accused me of forging documents and causing your father's death. That accusation is unjustified. It was Lord Kensu who produced forged papers to try and convince the Emperor that I was a traitor, hoping that he would be given Mitsukage Castle as a reward. His Imperial Majesty saw through the deception. Lord Kensu was to be beheaded publicly, but I pleaded for leniency. He was allowed to return home and die with dignity, by his own hand."

Lord Ankan reached inside his left sleeve and brought out a thick scroll.

"Here is an account of the trial, written by an imperial scribe," he said. "It includes the Emperor's proclamation of my innocence, and your father's guilt. I will leave it here for you to read."

The truth that Jimmu had once believed was rapidly vanishing, but he clung desperately to a final scrap.

"But I was told—" he began.

"You were told lies," said Lord Ankan. "Who lied about me?"

"Nichiren," Jimmu mumbled.

Lord Ankan started. "Araki Nichiren?"

"Yes."

Lord Ankan laughed bitterly.

"That explains much!" he exclaimed. "Araki Nichiren is my half-brother. My father did not marry his mother, and refused to acknowledge him as a member of the Choju family. Nichiren has hated me all his life. I knew he was a servant of Lord Kensu's, but he disappeared after his master's death. Do you know where he is?"

"Dead," said Jimmu. "I burned his body and scattered the ashes, but his voice is still alive in my mind."

Lord Ankan frowned deeply at this.

"Pardon me for asking, My Lord," Jimmu went on, "but what sort of man was my father?"

Lord Ankan stroked his beard and spoke slowly, choosing his words with care.

"Shimomura Kensu was arrogant, self-centred and hasty – as most young men are," he said. "He was impatient for wealth and power, and his ambition led him astray, but don't be too quick to condemn him. He did not live long enough to learn wisdom. The young frequently make mistakes. Your father paid dearly for his."

"And now I should be made to pay for mine!" declared Jimmu.

Lord Ankan gazed straight into Jimmu's eyes.

"It is plain to me that you were exploited by a deceitful man, who warped you to his own ends, but I cannot overlook your attempt on my life," he said. "If witnesses had been present, I would have no choice but to condemn you to death."

"My life is yours, to do with as you please, My Lord," Jimmu said humbly.

Lord Ankan grunted.

"At the moment, it pleases me that you should recover your health, and then continue your samurai training until I have decided on a suitable punishment for you," he said.

Jimmu was astounded.

"But, My Lord—" he gasped.

Lord Ankan sprang to his feet.

"You will do as I say!" he snapped. "A samurai must obey his lord in all things."

Jimmu bowed his head again.

"As you wish, My Lord," he said.

Chapter 19
Mitsukage Castle
ISE PROVINCE, WINTER 1572

After Lord Ankan left, Jimmu spent a long time reading through the scroll. The account of the trial was just as Lord Ankan had said. Nichiren had taken the facts, and turned them inside out to poison Jimmu's mind.

The old Jimmu, the one driven by a burning for revenge, was dead; the new Jimmu faced an uncertain future. Only one thing was certain: he would accept Lord Ankan's punishment without complaint, no matter what it might be.

Just as Jimmu reached this conclusion, the door of his room suddenly flew back, and Takeko appeared in the doorway. She was dressed all in white, her hair hung loose, and the expression in her eyes was terrifying.

"My father told me about you," she said in an

alarmingly quiet voice. "He took you in and fed you, and all the while you were plotting his death. I hate you. I wouldn't have treated you as my father has. I would have had you tortured with hot irons, and watched you die slowly. You tricked me into thinking you cared for me, but it was just a way of getting closer to my father, wasn't it? All you cared about was revenge. Don't dare to deny it! I won't believe anything you say!"

She spun on her heel, and stormed off along the corridor.

Jimmu made no attempt to stop her. He sensed that nothing he could say would make things right, and besides, he felt that he deserved Takeko's hatred.

Jimmu regained his strength and began training again. His instructor was a samurai named Ina Kyo, who had taken part in the raid on the Takeda camp. It took only a few sessions to demonstrate to Kyo that he had nothing to teach his pupil about the use of weapons, so he concentrated on unarmed combat, and building up Jimmu's stamina.

Kyo could do nothing for Jimmu's state of mind however. The daylight hours were filled with training, leaving Jimmu little opportunity to think about himself. Night-time was a different matter. Jimmu suffered from horrifically vivid dreams in which he was forced to fight Captain Muraki and Nichiren simultaneously, or found himself alone on a battlefield, facing the entire Takeda cavalry. The nightmares disturbed his sleep, so that he woke feeling just as tired as when he had lain down. Fatigue affected his concentration during training. Kyo noticed, and questioned Jimmu about it.

Jimmu responded angrily.

"I don't know why I can't concentrate!" he snapped. "Why can't you leave me alone?"

"Because Lord Ankan expects me to train you," replied Kyo. "Whatever is wrong, you had better sort it out in a hurry, Jimmu. You're starting to lose your edge. If you continue like this, I'll have to tell Lord Ankan that you'll never make the grade as a samurai."

This exchange shocked Jimmu, and he embarked on several lengthy and painful bouts of self-examination. The conclusions he drew were not comforting.

Lord Ankan had been right: Nichiren's lies had warped Jimmu's development, and turned him into someone he was not meant to be. The malign influences of his past still clung to him – his nightmares made that plain – and they would go on clinging to him until he discovered who he truly was.

Spring came early that year. Shortly after the thaw, a green haze of new growth showed in the farmland around the castle.

On a fine morning, Jimmu was summoned to Lord Ankan's private rooms. He guessed why, and resigned himself to whatever fate Lord Ankan had decided for him.

Lord Ankan was seated in a shaft of strong sunlight. The sound of birdsong drifted in through an opened shutter.

"You are better, I trust?" Lord Ankan enquired, after Jimmu's preliminary bow.

"My body is much better, thank you, My Lord, but my spirit is troubled," Jimmu replied frankly.

"So Ina Kyo has informed me, and I believe I can

explain why," said Lord Ankan. "The ghosts of the dead still haunt you, and you will never lay them to rest while you remain in Mitsukage Castle. You are too close to me, and the memory of your old hatred."

"Your Lordship means to banish me?" ventured Jimmu.

"I mean to send you on a samurai pilgrimage," Lord Ankan said. "You will travel the country, seek out great sword-masters and learn all you can from them. You will also visit shrines and pray for guidance. When you are purged of your past, you will return here."

Jimmu was mystified.

"Return, My Lord?" he said.

Lord Ankan nodded.

"I have spent many hours meditating on your story, and I cannot help concluding that my father was partly to blame for what happened to you. If he had treated Nichiren less harshly..." Lord Ankan sighed. "Well, what is done cannot be undone, but it may be atoned for. Since the Emperor has decreed that the family name of Shimomura no longer exists, I am prepared to adopt you into my family, once your pilgrimage is over."

Jimmu felt close to tears. Choju Ankan, the man he had been brought up to hate, was offering him more than his own father ever had. Jimmu had discovered the truth at last, and his inner and outer world had become one.

"I owe you so much, My Lord," he said. "I swear to devote myself totally to your service. While we both live, I will be your samurai. Tomorrow, at dawn, I will set out on my pilgrimage."

Jimmu woke before first light the following morning. He dressed in a plain cotton kimono, and secured his sword with a black sash tied around his waist. Then he went down to the main gate, where he found Kambei waiting.

"Thought you could sneak off without saying goodbye to your old nursemaid, did you?" Kambei scolded. "Think again, young man!"

Jimmu laughed in surprise.

"How did you know I was leaving?" he asked.

"Word gets around," said Kambei, shrugging with one shoulder. "In a place like this, you can't break wind at night without everybody knowing about it the next day."

Kambei reached inside his kimono and withdrew a small leather purse, which he offered to Jimmu.

"What is it?" Jimmu said.

"Sergeant Hankei instructed me to make a collection for you," explained Kambei.

Jimmu frowned in disapproval.

"Go on, take it!" insisted Kambei. "Even pilgrims need to eat, and sleep with a roof over their heads sometimes. Consider it a loan that you can repay when you come back."

Jimmu smiled, and accepted the purse.

"Thanks, Kambei," he said, "and thank the others for me."

Kambei tugged at the lobe of his left ear.

"I was going to wish you good luck, but you don't need it, because anyone can see you're going to be a fine samurai before long," he said. "So I'll give you a bit of advice instead. Take the road to Zato."

"Why?"

"Oh, I had a dream that you went that way, and met with good fortune," Kambei said airily.

"Do you often have dreams about me, Kambei?" teased Jimmu.

"Only when I can't help it," Kambei said. "Remember, the road to Zato!"

The sun rose, and its light reflected off the dew that had formed overnight, making necklaces of the spiders' webs in the bushes on the roadside.

Jimmu kept up a steady pace and met no other travellers, until, after a half-hour's walking, he heard hoofbeats approaching from behind. While stepping aside so that the horse could pass, Jimmu glanced idly over his shoulder. He saw Takeko, riding a dapple grey mare. Takeko was dressed as a boy, in a cotton top, breeches, and a straw hat. She reined the horse to a halt, and slid out of the saddle.

Jimmu bowed.

"Have you come to gloat, My Lady?" he said. "How pleased you must be that I'm leaving your father's castle."

"Don't presume to know what my feelings are," Takeko said frostily.

Jimmu bowed again.

"Forgive me, My Lady. You're right," he said. "Why should you feel anything for me but contempt?"

Misery showed in Takeko's eyes.

"Please, Jimmu, let's not say goodbye like this!"

she said. "I had to swallow a lot of pride before I could come after you."

"The last time we spoke, you told me that you hated me," Jimmu reminded her.

"I was angry with you then," said Takeko.

"And you're not angry with me now?"

"I don't know what I am!" Takeko groaned. "I was angry with you, then I missed you, and I'm going to miss you even more, and — you mix me up!"

Jimmu relented. He knew exactly how Takeko felt, because he felt the same way himself.

"I'm sorry," he said. "I don't mean to."

"I know you don't, but it doesn't make things any easier!" Takeko took a deep breath to steady herself. "What are you going to do, Jimmu? How will you live?"

"I have a little money," said Jimmu. "When it runs out, I'll do odd jobs, find work as a nightwatchman or a guard. I'll get by."

"You have to promise me that you'll come back," Takeko said.

"Ladies of your rank shouldn't—" began Jimmu.

"You sound like my grandmother!" Takeko

growled. "None of that matters any longer. Once father adopts you, you'll be a member of the family."

"So we'll be like brother and sister?" said Jimmu.

"Like really, really distant cousins," Takeko corrected him. "Here." She fumbled with the pouch at her side, and brought out the red jade horse she had bought at the market in Sakura. The horse had been attached to a leather cord. "Wear this around your neck, to remind you of me."

"I won't need to be reminded," said Jimmu. "I'll think about you every day."

"Of course you will!" Takeko agreed. "But wear it anyway."

Jimmu took the horse from her, and slipped his head through the loop of the cord. As he did, a thought occurred to him. "Did you order Kambei to suggest that I went this way?"

"It wasn't an order, just a suggestion," Takeko said. "I think we've taken up enough of each other's time, don't you? I can't stand drawn-out goodbyes."

She mounted her horse.

"Takeko?" said Jimmu. "What if Lord Ankan marries you off to a rich nobleman while I'm away?"

"He won't!" Takeko snorted.

"How do you know?"

"Because I won't let him!" Takeko said fiercely. She dug her heels into the mare's flanks, and the horse galloped off in the direction of Mitsukage Castle.

Jimmu did not watch Takeko ride away. He set out towards Zato, certain that he was doing the right thing.

No more listening to voices from the past, he vowed to himself. From now on, I'll make my own decisions.

Jimmu strode purposefully along the road, and did not look behind him.

Usborne Quicklinks

For links to websites where you can find out more about how samurai lived and trained, examine samurai armour or read about the history of Japan, go to the Usborne Quicklinks Website at www.usborne-quicklinks.com and type the keywords "way of the warrior".

Internet safety

When using the internet, make sure you follow these safety guidelines:

- Ask an adult's permission before using the internet.
- Never give out personal information, such as your name, address or telephone number.
- If a website asks you to type in your name or e-mail address, check with an adult first.
- If you receive an e-mail from someone you don't know, don't reply to it.